10 Steps to Fulfilling Your Divine Destiny:

A Christian Woman's Guide to Learning and Living God's Plan for Her

Marnie L. Pehrson

2nd Edition
© 2002 Marnie L. Pehrson
All rights reserved.
Published by C.E.S. Business Consultants
Tel: 706-866-2295

ISBN 0-9676162-1-2

*To Greg, the love of my life and the shoulder
that's always there for me to lean on.*

Table of Contents

Acknowledgement

Many thanks goes to those who have helped me along my spiritual journey and in discovering the 10 steps to learning and living your divine destiny, and to those who have helped me organize the information in book form:

To my parents, Jack and Betty Morton for always encouraging me in the pursuit of my dreams – for my mother's faithfulness and my father's listening ear. To my sister, Lisa Kline, who helped instill in me a love for spiritual things.

To Alanna Webb, Karon Thackston, my mother, and Debbie Williams for reviewing the original manuscript, and especially for Alanna's book preparation help and Debbie's brainstorming sessions and constant support in encouraging me to write the book.

To my dear friend Suzanne Moore for her "peeling the onion analogy" and for our "porch talks" from which much of the material for this book was distilled.

To my loyal readers and visitors at SheLovesGod.com who encouraged me and helped me believe that my writing could touch lives.

Lastly, an eternity of thanks to my dear friend and coach, Jenette Zubero, for being the angel the Lord sent to help me discover my own divine destiny. Words cannot express the gratitude I feel in my heart for her continued support, her ever-listening ear, her willingness to ask with a sincere heart, and her ability to hear the voice of the Master. Without Jenette, there would be no SheLovesGod.com, and this book would not exist.

Introduction

Have you ever said to yourself, "I'd love to do great things with my life, but I'm just too busy, too untalented, too ordinary, too afraid, too anything but extraordinary"? Inside this book you'll learn the answers to:

- Who are you?
- Where did you come from?
- What is this life all about?
- If you could reach your full potential and remove all roadblocks that stand in your way, what could you be and do?
- If with God, all things are possible and He can help you reach this potential, what currently stands in your way of a closer relationship with Him?
- And how do you draw close enough for Him to reveal His plan for your life?

In this book you will learn how to unlock your full God-given potential. No matter your denomination, beliefs or background, the greatest thing you can do in this life is to come unto Christ, for in doing so, He will uncover your soul. Jesus Christ transforms lives – it's what He does. If you will let Him, if you will come unto Him, He can make you happier and more fulfilled than you could be if you pursued any other course.

Today's Christian women are sleeping giants, and when we finally awake and arise, we will join the ranks of Esther, Ruth, Mary and Martha. Be among those who wake up! This book will outline ten steps that will lead you to a closer relationship with Jesus Christ and thus lead you to your full potential. You may have already taken some of the steps, but they could bear repeating. As a matter of fact, these steps should be repeated throughout your life. Coming to Christ is a constant, never-ending process. We never reach a point at which we "arrive" and thus need not keep following Him. We must continually strive to follow in His footsteps and one day we will look up and see that He has led us straight to the throne of God. So let's get started on your quest to discovering and fulfilling your God-given mission!

Chapter 1
Learn Who You Are

Imagine for a moment that you have just received a blow to the head. Upon awakening in a hospital in a foreign country, you are unable to remember who you are and have no recollection of your life, your beliefs or your background.

A police officer enters your room and explains that he has found identification on you indicating that you have been traveling alone. An information search reveals that you have made many mistakes in this foreign country and are heavily in debt. You have been in and out of trouble your whole life. There's no evidence that you have any family. The officer says he's heard of the harsh, unforgiving employer who has sent you to work from another country. He insists that your employer will undoubtedly be very angry with you should you attempt to return to your native land.

- How would you feel about yourself upon learning this information?
- How hopeful do you think you would be?
- What kind of feelings would you have about the possibility of returning to your home country?

The next day another police officer comes to visit you. After a thorough search, he discovers a bag of your belongings near the crime scene. As you look through your belongings, you discover that you are a princess – a daughter of a famous king from a wonderful country where everyone wants to live. Your father, the king, is a forgiving, loving individual. He, not an employer, has sent you here to perform a special mission. You possess unique talents that suit you for fulfilling this mission.

Although you have made mistakes while visiting this country, your oldest brother has agreed to pay all your debts if you will resume the mission and do your best to fulfill it.

Accompanying you on your mission are brothers, sisters, family, friends and other guides who can help you accomplish your mission. You also have a personal companion to go on the journey to guide and comfort you when you encounter challenges.

Your father, the king, has provided you with guidebooks that will help you rediscover who you are, who your father is, and your purpose. He is always available for you to call and will listen to you. He is looking forward to your return with open arms. Now, what are your feelings?

- How would you feel about yourself after learning this information?
- How hopeful would you be?
- What kind of feelings would you have about the possibility of returning to your home country?
- How interested would you be in reading the guidebooks you were given?
- How long would it take before you tried to communicate with those who are known to be your friends and family?
- How long would it take for you to call your father?

On both days you still had amnesia, but what made such a profound difference between day 1 and day 2? Why did you have so much more hope on the second day than on the first?

- You knew you were really the child of a famous, loving king.
- Even though you had debts your elder brother had agreed to pay for them if you stayed committed to the mission.
- You had family/friends who cared about you.

- You knew why you were here – you had a unique mission to fulfill and possessed the talents and the ability needed to accomplish this mission.
- You had instruction books and guides to help you along the way.
- You had a constant companion to personally guide you.
- You had the ability to call your father at any time.
- You knew you had a loving father to return to.

How many of us live our lives as if it's day one when the truth is soon to be discovered on day two? Just as this little story suggests, the first order of business is for you to understand who you are, who your Father is, and your true relationship to Him. You must come to understand that there is great potential within you. None of us truly sees our own magnitude, but God does. He knows who you are, who you have always been and who you can yet become. If you will come unto Him and strive to live His teachings, you can begin to catch a glimpse of His wonderful plan for your life, and work toward living it. Great joy and peace will be the result.

Where Did You Come From?

Before we discuss the ten steps for learning and living God's plan for you, let's lay a little groundwork and discuss who you are, where you came from and why you're here. You are a composite being. You are comprised of a spirit and a body. Have you ever had the feeling that you have always existed? That your birth was not the beginning and that death will not be the end? This is a very common feeling for many people and perhaps it is because it is true! According to the Bible, your spirit has been around much longer than your body has. As a matter of fact, it was around before the world was even formed! Look at this passage from Proverbs 8:22-31:

The Lord possessed me in the beginning of his way, before his works of old. I was set up from everlasting, from the beginning, or ever the earth was.

When there were no depths, I was brought forth; when there were no fountains abounding with water. Before the mountains were settled, before the hills was I brought forth:

While as yet he had not made the earth, nor the fields, nor the highest part of the dust of the world. When he prepared the heavens, I was there: when he set a compass upon the face of the depth:

When he established the clouds above: when he strengthened the fountains of the deep: When he gave the sea his decree, that the waters should not pass his commandment: when he appointed the foundations of the earth. Then I was by him, as one brought up with him: and I was daily his delight, rejoicing always before him; Rejoicing in the habitable part of his earth; and my delight were with the sons of men.

Before the foundations of the world, we were with God. As a daughter of God, you were His delight. We were with each other. Our Heavenly Father and Jesus Christ's "delight *was* with the sons *(and we could add daughters)* of men." Another verse that tells the source of our spirits is Ecclesiastes 12: 7: "Then shall the dust return to the earth as it was: and the spirit shall return unto God who gave it." You came from His presence.

William Wordsworth summarized it this way:

Our birth is but a sleep and a forgetting
The soul that rises with us, our life's star
Hath had elsewhere its setting,
And cometh from afar:
Not in entire forgetfulness,
And not in utter nakedness.
But trailing clouds of glory do we come
From God, who is our home.

Who Are You?

You are a daughter of God. God is the Father of your spirit. Hebrews 12:9 teaches us, "we have had fathers of our flesh which corrected us, and we gave them reverence: shall we not much rather be in subjection unto the Father of spirits, and live?" And Acts 17:28-29 says, "For in Him we live, and move, and have our being; as certain also of your own poets have said, For we are also His offspring. Forasmuch then as we are the offspring of God, we ought not to think that the Godhead is like unto gold, or silver, or stone, graven by art and man's device."

Genesis 1:26-27 explains that you are made in God's image. You are made in His likeness. There is a piece of you that is divine. As mentioned earlier, you are a composite being comprised of a spirit (which came from the presence of God) and a body that is earthly and made of the elements of the earth.

Each of us fights a constant inward struggle between things spiritual and things carnal. The body is the "natural man" (or woman) described by Paul as receiving "not the things of the Spirit of God: for they are foolishness unto him *(or her)*; neither can he *(or she)* know them, because they are spiritually discerned." (1 Corinthians 2:14)

So here we are, spirit children of our Heavenly Father, tied to bodies that have no mechanism for discerning spiritual things. Two pieces of us are vying for control over what we do. If the spirit wins the battle, then we hear and act upon spiritual things, and we begin to hear and see things from God's perspective. If the body wins, it follows its own cravings and leads us into foolish and dangerous paths because it cannot hear the warning voice of the Holy Spirit who is trying to communicate with our spirit.

This is why Satan and his minions are so focused on getting the world to be engrossed in sexual immorality, drugs, and alcohol. These things gratify bodily lusts and appetites, shutting down communication with the spirit. When the body is running rampant and out of control, the subtle spiritual side of our being is drowned out by a tumult of distractions and noise.

Let me relate an ordinary incident that drove this point home for me. We live on some land we share with my sister's family who has a house next door. We lead a peaceful, quiet life (other than the raucous of children underfoot). I rarely leave the property other than to go to church or the grocery store since all my business is on the Internet.

One Friday evening my husband and I were invited to a party in downtown Chattanooga hosted by a pharmaceutical company affiliated with my husband's office. As we entered the restaurant, a burst of sites, sounds and smells enveloped us. The restaurant had a vaulted warehouse-type ceiling that reverberated rather than absorbed the noise. The only seats we could find were located next to a couple of people who ate very little but drank and smoked plenty. I began to cough and sputter and lean my head away as far as possible without looking conspicuous. Between the noise and the smoking I could hear my inner voice crying out, "Sensory Overload! Sensory Overload!" My immediate desire was to leave as fast as possible, but I knew I couldn't. After a while I adjusted to the noise level and found a new place to sit with cleaner air.

This is a good illustration of how our spirits feel when they are smothered by worldly cares, concerns or stimulants. Our spirits are sensitive instruments that need peaceful and quiet contemplation to function properly. Our spiritual sides can easily be overloaded, and when exposed to too much noise, too many worldly distractions, they retreat or become drowned out. If we let bodily desires and appetites take control, what is the likelihood of the body listening to or even hearing the "still small voice" as it attempts to guide us to safety and peace?

"Inspiration comes more easily in peaceful settings. Such words as quiet, still, peaceable, Comforter abound in the scriptures... The world grows increasingly noisy. Clothing and grooming and conduct are looser and sloppier and more disheveled. Raucous music, with obscene lyrics blasted through amplifiers while lights flash psychedelic colors, characterizes the drug culture. Variations of these things are gaining wide acceptance and influence over the youth...

"This trend to more noise, more excitement, more contention, less restraint, less dignity, less formality is not coincidental nor innocent nor harmless. The first order issued by the commander mounting a military invasion is the jamming of the channels of communication of those he intends to conquer. Irreverence suits the purposes of the adversary by obstructing the delicate channels of revelation in both mind and spirit." [1]

Each of us needs quiet times to contemplate, meditate and feed our spirits through prayer and scripture study. Just as our body needs to be fed, so does our spirit.

Why Are You Here?

Why did you even need to come to earth? Why do you need a body? Why couldn't you have just stayed a spirit? Think about it, what are some things that you would be unable to do without a body?

* You couldn't have children or learn all the things that are to be learned from parenthood.
* You couldn't experience the touch or feel of other people.
* You couldn't give a friend a hug when they needed it most.
* You couldn't feel the softness of a kiss on your baby's cheek.
* You couldn't have as close a bond with other people such as your husband or children without being able to touch, hug or kiss them.
* You couldn't learn lessons that can only be learned by overcoming the body and mastering bodily appetites and passions.
* You couldn't experience full joy, because so much of joy is a physical sensation.

Coming to this earth and gaining a body is an integral part of God's plan for you. But there's more than that. God literally has a plan or a mission for your life. You have been placed here for a very special purpose – to fulfill a divine mission. Yet sadly, so few of us ever even realize this or seek it out.

In Jeremiah 1:4-5 the word of the Lord came to Jeremiah and told him, "Before I formed thee in the belly I knew thee; and before thou camest forth out of the womb I sanctified thee, and I ordained thee a prophet unto the nations."

Just as Jeremiah was chosen before he was born and foreordained to be a prophet of God, each of us is here on earth at this time to fulfill a very special purpose – to fulfill a divine mission. It could be said of us as it was of Esther who was called to save her people from execution: "and who knoweth whether thou art come to the kingdom for such a time as this?" (Esther 4:14) God has a plan for us that cannot be frustrated by our lack of talent, but He has given us our free will to choose to accept His plan for us or not. If we choose to throw it aside and wallow in self-doubt and self-pity, then not only do we lose precious blessings, but also everything and everyone we would have touched for good will suffer.

Chapter 2
Come Unto Christ

There's a remarkable story in Matthew chapter 4 that we often take for granted because we've heard it so much. Simon and Andrew had heard that Jesus was the Messiah. One day, Jesus was walking by the Sea of Galilee and saw them casting a net into the sea. And He said to them, "Follow me, and I will make you fishers of men." Straightway they left their nets and followed him.

Imagine that! You've heard that this man is the Messiah. He comes to you and asks you to leave your work, leave your family and follow Him. He wants you to go with Him around the countryside to teach, and says you'll do greater things with your life than just the day-to-day grind. He'll make you fishers of men. He'll make you someone who can lead souls to God, who can be an instrument in the hands of God in transforming lives and leading them to the light.

Would you believe Him? Even if you believed He was the Son of God, might you still feel inclined to say, "Yeah, but He doesn't know me. There's nothing special about me. I can't be useful to Him. I'm just an ordinary person with a lot of problems and hang-ups."

But Jesus took these ordinary men, not scripture scholars, but ordinary fishermen and made them His apostles, men of God with power to act, heal, and teach in His name. That is one of the most powerful messages of Jesus Christ – that He can take ordinary people and transform them into extraordinary instruments in His hands. And this doesn't just apply to Simon and Andrew; it applies to you and me.

One might also say, "But what about my life?" What of Simon and Andrew? Did their lives change when they dropped their nets and followed Jesus Christ? Of course! Jesus even changed Simon's name to Peter. They were never the same again. That had to have been scary for them at that moment of decision. I wonder if they even understood how much their lives would change? Did they know that they would work mighty miracles in His name? Did they even begin to comprehend that they would be instruments in bringing thousands to the feet of Jesus Christ where they would find salvation for their souls? I doubt it.

"Whom do men say that I the Son of man am?" asked Jesus of His disciples. They answered, "Some say that thou art John the Baptist: some Elias, and others Jeremiah or one of the other prophets." Jesus replied, "But whom say ye that I am?" Simon Peter answered, "Thou art the Christ, the Son of the living God."

Jesus answered and said to Peter, "Blessed art thou, Simon Barjona: for flesh and blood hath not revealed it unto thee, but my Father which is in heaven." (Matthew 16:13-17) John the Revelator explained, "the testimony of Jesus is the spirit of prophecy." (Revelation 19:10). When we have a testimony of Jesus, we are exercising the spirit of prophecy – a gift of the Spirit (see 1 Corinthians 12).

Even though Peter had the spirit of prophecy to declare that Jesus is the Son of the living God, the Lord later told Peter at the Last Supper, "Simon, Simon, behold Satan hath desired to have you that he may sift you as wheat. But I have prayed for thee that thy faith fail not: and **when thou art converted, strengthen thy brethren**." Even though Peter had a testimony of the divinity of Jesus Christ, he was not yet converted. According to the thesaurus, *converted* means transformed, recreated or changed.

There is a difference between knowing the path and walking the path. There is a difference between knowing, doing and becoming. The gospel of Jesus Christ invites us to *become* someone new. As Paul said, "Therefore if any man be in Christ, he is a new creature: old things are passed away; behold, all things are become new." (2 Corinthians 5:17)

When we drop our old lives, throw down our nets and follow Jesus Christ, we start on a path that can seem quite scary. We may feel like we're leaving not only our old habits behind, but also sometimes even our very selves behind. But it is always worth it. The person He transforms us into is more beautiful, exciting, vibrant and happy than anything we could have become on our own. *And isn't it only fitting, only logical, that God can do so much more with a life than we can do with it ourselves?*

God takes ordinary people and transforms them into extraordinary instruments in His hands. No matter how boring, untalented or ordinary we feel we are, Jesus Christ, if we let Him, will transform us into mighty instruments for good that can make a miraculous difference in the world around us.

Jesus invites us all to come unto Him. So how do we in the 21st century come unto Christ? How do we go from having mere testimonies that He lives and that His gospel message is true to being truly converted such that our hearts are changed? There are 10 steps to this process of conversion to Jesus Christ. And these 10 steps are the same steps you will need to take to discover your God-given mission. These steps involve the process Jesus described in Matthew 11:28-30,

"Come unto me all ye that labor and are heavy laden, and I will give you rest. Take my yoke upon you, and learn of me; for I am meek and lowly in heart: and ye shall find rest unto your souls. For my yoke is easy and my burden is light."

For many, the message of this passage seems impossible. Why would it be an easy yoke when Christ asks so much of us? We often feel so overwhelmed with all the commandments and the *should's* that we feel obligated to accomplish. So how can He say that His "burden is light"?

In the following chapters, you will learn how this is possible and how it can happen for you. Let's begin your journey through the 10 steps to conversion which will not only lead you to Christ, but also to discovering the divine destiny the Lord has in store for you as a daughter of God.

Bear in mind that your divine destiny is a way of life. It's not a onetime destination. And although compelling, it's not something that occurs without effort on your part. Think of these ten steps as a staircase. You climb this staircase a step at a time, but sometimes you'll linger on a step for a season. At other times, you may feel as if you're leaping up the staircase, taking two and three steps at a time. It is also possible to slip back down the steps if you don't continue to remember and strive toward following Christ.

As you climb these steps, you'll soon discover that there are several flights to this staircase. You'll walk these steps again and again as you work toward reaching new spiritual levels. Apply the steps as needed whenever you find yourself in growth seasons of your life. I would even venture to say that these steps will continue to be the pattern beyond this life and into the next.

Step 1: Desire to Know Him

The summer I was eight, my father spent hours trying to teach me how to dive. I would run up to the edge of the pool with all the motions of diving in, only to stop short at the very last second and not follow through. No matter how elaborate my theatrics, both he and I knew that the final step of entering the water wasn't going to happen. I was terrified of the water, and frankly I had no desire to plunge headfirst into that pool.

My dad tried pep talks and demonstrations, reminding me that I knew how to swim. But nothing helped. The thought of falling air-born into the water petrified me. Finally, one afternoon near the end of the summer, without warning, he scooped me up into his arms and threw me into the water. Shocked, I began to swim, made my way to the edge of the pool and climbed out. Irritated, but unharmed, I learned that the world would not end should I fall into a pool of water. His method, although startling, helped me overcome my fears, and I did indeed learn to dive. Had he never thrown me in, I probably never would have learned. I was stuck – blocked by a wall of fear that began at the edge of the pool. Although my fears were somewhat overcome through this incident, it would still be years before I developed any real desire to dive without being coaxed by someone else.

No one can give you a desire, but they can teach you. They can show you the way and make it seem appealing. However the desire, in the end, must come from within.

The first step to coming unto Christ is a desire to learn of Him, to understand Him, to be like Him. We have to be willing to experiment with His words, and exercise a particle of faith, even if all we can do is have the desire to believe. We can then allow that desire to work in us until we believe enough to experiment upon His words. The fact that you are reading this book shows that in some measure you have a desire to follow the Lord and to fulfill His plan for your life. Perhaps the Lord has at some point thrown you into the water to help you come to this point. Or perhaps you have come to it on your own. Whichever way the desire comes, it must eventually be your choice.

If you seek the Lord you will find Him, if you "seek Him with all thy heart and with all thy soul." (Deuteronomy. 4:29). "Love the Lord thy God with all thy heart, and with all thy soul and with all thy mind." (Matthew 22:37). Solomon was advised, "know thou the God of thy father, and serve Him with a perfect heart and with a willing mind: for the LORD searcheth all hearts, and understandeth all the imaginations of the thoughts: if thou seek Him, He will be found of thee; but if thou forsake Him, He will cast thee off for ever." (I Chronicles 28:9). It's no accident that your heart was mentioned first, for where your treasure is, there will your heart be also.

"Notice that He said nothing about how gorgeous or thin, educated or affluent we must be. He simply asks for our hearts and our will, because that's all we have to give Him. Everything else is already His. Ultimately we will become what we give our hearts to, for we are shaped by what we desire and seek after. If we love the Lord such that our hearts are changed, His image will fill our countenances."[2]

Step 2: Ask

Are Answers Really Out There?

We all experience confusion in our lives at one time or another. We all have questions or concerns with which we grapple. We may be faced with a major challenge that requires a decision on our part, or perhaps we are considering a career change or a move for our family. Sometimes we feel tugged to grow spiritually or move in a different direction entirely in our relationship with God, but aren't sure in which direction to travel. Whatever our dilemma, it all begins with a question. The old saying *necessity is the mother of invention* could be rephrased as *questions are the mother of inspiration*. If we never ask, we will never receive. If we never knock, the door won't be opened. If we don't seek, we won't find. So as painful and confusing as our moments of indecision may be, they are the beginning of greater things to come if we will diligently seek, knock and ask.

Many people go through this life believing that there are no answers, that we're just here to do the best we can and whatever path we take is just fine... sort of a *go with the flow* philosophy. They believe that God doesn't intend for us to have answers to our perplexing questions about life, about Him, or about how we should live. And it is true that there are some questions that may not be answered until the next life, but I believe that this is more the exception than the rule when it comes to important matters that are dear to our hearts. Why else would there be over two dozen verses in the New Testament alone that admonish us to ask with the promise that the Lord will answer?

If we are not meant to have and to know the path that is right for us, why then does Psalm 37:23 tell us that "The steps of a *good* man are ordered by the LORD?" So when we lack wisdom, direction and answers, what should we do? James 1:5-6 provides the answer, "If any of you lack wisdom, let him ask of God, that giveth to all men liberally, and upbraideth not; and it shall be given him. But let him ask in faith, nothing wavering. For he that wavereth is like a wave of the sea driven with the wind and tossed."

What does it mean to "ask in faith, nothing wavering?" *Expect an answer*. The Lord promises to answer, so we must have faith in Him, listen and wait expectantly for His answer. Sometimes the answer comes immediately. Sometimes it comes later in the day. But perhaps the reason why many people believe we can't receive answers is that they often don't come immediately. Sometimes we must wait weeks, months or even years to gain the wisdom we need or the answer for which we asked. Isaiah 28:13 explains, "But the word of the Lord was unto them precept upon precept, precept upon precept; line upon line, line upon line; here a little, and there a little."

Has someone ever turned on a bright light over your head while you were sleeping? What does that do to your eyes? It's shocking isn't it? It hurts because it forces your eyes to immediately readjust to the influx of light. Usually your initial response is to duck your head under the covers where it's nice and dark. I believe that spiritually speaking, the Lord has to train most of us *line upon line* and *precept upon precept* because the shock of the full force of His light would overwhelm us, sending us fleeing into the comfort of the darkness. "Wait on the Lord: be of good courage, and He shall strengthen thine heart: wait, I say, on the Lord." (Psalms 27: 14).

As the Lord feeds us *precept upon precept and line upon line* our job is to accept and live true to the light and knowledge that we're being given. In Matthew 13:10-16, Jesus' disciples asked Him why He spoke in parables. He answered, "Because it is given unto you to know the mysteries of the kingdom of heaven, but to them it is not given. For whosoever hath, to him shall be given, and he shall have more abundance: but whosoever hath not, from him shall be taken away even that he hath. Therefore speak I to them in parables: because they seeing see not; and hearing they hear not, neither do they understand..."

"For this people's heart is waxed gross, and their ears are dull of hearing, and their eyes they have closed; lest at any time they should see with their eyes, and hear with their ears, and should understand with their heart, and should be converted, and I should heal them. But blessed are your eyes, for they see: and your ears, for they hear."

If we are not willing to see, hear and do what the Lord tells us, how can we expect to receive more? If we close our minds and shut off the possibilities – shut off the mysteries, can we ever expect to gain the wisdom we lack? Remember, that "the wisdom of the world is foolishness with God." (1 Corinthians 3:19). And the opposite of that is true as well... sometimes the wisdom of God looks foolish to the world. To paraphrase Proverbs 3:5-6, we must, "trust in the LORD with all *our* heart; and lean not *upon our* own understanding. In all *our* ways acknowledge Him, and He shall direct *our* paths."

Is simply asking enough?

Simply asking is not always enough; we must ask intelligently. There are guidelines for asking that yield greater success:

Ask in faith, nothing wavering

Continuing in James 1:6-8, "But let him ask in faith, nothing wavering. For he that wavereth is like a wave of the sea driven with the wind and tossed. For let not that man think that he shall receive any thing of the Lord. A double minded man is unstable in all his ways." So unwavering faith is important.

How then can we be double minded in our prayers? What if we pray for help to overcome a temptation, but really have no intention of not giving into it when it presents itself again? A request such as "Please help me not to get drunk Friday night" and then planning a night at the bar with some friends would most definitely be double minded.

Another way to be double minded is to not make up our minds. The Lord likes us to use the minds He gave us. He likes us to prayerfully think through a dilemma from all sides, come to a decision that we feel would be the best and then come to Him with our best choice. Then when we pray we can specifically ask Him, "After studying the alternatives, I think I should take the new job offer at XYZ company. Please let me know if this is the right decision, and help me to have a feeling of peace if this is the right choice. Please help me to feel uneasy or unsure if this is not the right choice." The Holy Spirit is the Comforter. When we make a clear, single-minded choice in faith and come to the Lord with it, if it is the correct decision, the Holy Spirit will give us a feeling of peace as His seal of approval. If His approval is absent, we will feel dark, depressed, confused or uneasy – basically experiencing discomfort and a lack of peace.

If you don't ask, you won't get an answer

It sounds obvious, but if you don't ask the question, you won't get an answer. There are questions that the Lord would love to answer for us, but if we don't ever ask Him – if our minds are closed, he's not going to force the answers upon us. This is explained in John 16:24 where Jesus said, "Hitherto have ye asked nothing in my name: ask, and ye shall receive; that your joy may be full." If we don't ask – if we are not hungering and thirsting after truth, then we cannot expect to receive a fullness of joy.

Have you ever noticed that Jesus always admonished us to "Come" unto Him? He didn't say, "Wait there and I'll come to you." Instead He declared, "O Jerusalem, Jerusalem… how often would I have gathered thy children together, even as a hen gathereth her chickens under her wings, and ye would not." (Matthew 23:37). Have you ever seen a hen gather her chickens before a storm? She doesn't run around the barnyard rounding them up. She stands in one spot, raises her wings and the chicks run under the shelter of her protective body. So Jesus is saying, "I'm here ready and willing to shelter you in my loving arms, but you have to come unto me." In Jerusalem's case, He would have loved to have protected them and showed them His love, but they would not come.

There are blessings and knowledge that the Lord is willing and waiting to give us if we will but come to Him and ask. This is why in the scriptures we are repeatedly told, "For every one that asketh receiveth; and he that seeketh findeth; and to him that knocketh it shall be opened" (Luke 11:10). The Lord *does* hear and answer prayers.

Asking involves searching and pondering

The Lord told the Israelites to "inquire, and make search, and ask diligently" (Deuteronomy 13:14) so that they would know what to do. Effective asking involves searching and diligence. If we search His word, we will find the answers we seek. We can also search by talking with other faithful followers of Christ to gain better understanding or to learn how they handled similar situations. We ask diligently by continuing to study, ponder and pray. An indicator of our desire for something is how hard and long we are willing to raise our petitions to the Lord for help and understanding.

Ask for what is right

James 4:3 says, "Ye ask, and receive not, because ye ask amiss, that ye may consume it upon your lusts." It does no good to pray for calamity to befall your neighbor or to pray for riches, honor or privileges simply to satisfy your own pride and vanity. God does not answer those kinds of prayers. We also should never pray for something that violates His commandments.

Keep the commandments

"And whatsoever we ask, we receive of Him, because we keep His commandments, and do those things that are pleasing in His sight." (I John 3:22). Christ taught, "If ye love me, keep my commandments" (John 14:15). When we prove to the Lord that we love Him by keeping His commandments and doing those things that are pleasing in His sight, He is much more inclined to hear and answer our prayers. Think about it, if you have two children and one is obedient and does what he is told and the other complains and rarely keeps the rules of your home, which one would you be more inclined to reward with extra treats?

In summary, if we remember to ask in faith, believing that we will receive, nothing wavering, with diligence in keeping His commandments, surely the Lord will make known unto us His will and will hear and answer our prayers. We will gain "treasures of wisdom and knowledge" (Col. 2:3)

My challenge to you is to give your heart to "seek and search out by wisdom concerning all things that are done under heaven" (Ecclesiastes. 1: 13) "for God giveth to a man (or woman) that *which* is good in His sight: wisdom, and knowledge, and joy." (Ecclesiastes. 2: 26). I testify to you that the answers *are* out there! Ask, seek, and knock with faith and persistence, and open your mind to God's infinite possibilities.

Step 3: Learn of Me

I have had numerous opportunities to discuss God with people of diverse backgrounds and denominations. One of the most common comments I have heard is "I want to get closer to the Lord." My standard reply is "Are you reading your scriptures every day?" Most of the time the answer is "No, I need to work on that" or "No, do you think that would help?"

I have been somewhat amazed by that response... not that most of us don't need to work on being more consistent with our daily scripture study, but that people don't equate scripture study with growing closer to the Lord.

If you wanted to get to know a neighbor, a relative or a friend, wouldn't you spend time listening to what they have to say? Jesus said, "Take my yoke upon you, and **learn of me**; for I am meek and lowly in heart: and ye shall find rest unto your souls." (Matthew 11: 29) The scriptures are one of today's most important sources for information about God and of what He has to say to you. The Savior said it in this way, "Search the scriptures; for in them... ye have eternal life: and they are they which testify of me." (John 5:39) If searching the scriptures leads to eternal life, then it most definitely leads us to God! Notice He uses the word *search*. He does not say read or scan. Searching the scriptures implies:

- pondering and really contemplating a passage or verse
- reading the passage over several times
- cross-referencing and looking up similar verses
- studying how you might apply the passage to your own life; and putting the scripture passage to work in your thoughts and actions.

Many of us were never taught how to properly study the scriptures. For those who haven't been taught, it can be overwhelming. Many think that reading their scriptures involves starting from the beginning and reading cover to cover; this can become overwhelming. It doesn't have to be. Scripture study should be enjoyable and enlightening. So, I'd like to share with you some of the things that help me to be more consistent in my scripture study and get more from it.

What to Study

If reading cover to cover overwhelms you, instead start with the four gospels: Matthew, Mark, Luke and John. These make for easy reading and are the words of the Savior Himself. I've found more answers to my prayers and life problems in the words of the Master than anywhere else. Other books of the Bible that are particularly insightful and easy to read are Genesis, Job, Psalms, Proverbs, Ruth, Acts, and James.

You might also choose to research a theme. For example, this week you might study about prayer looking up in your concordance all the verses relating to prayer. Next week you might study about adversity, and use your concordance to look up all the verses about adversity and life challenges. Purchase a set of scriptures containing a good index at your local Christian bookstore.

When to study

If you can make it a ritualistic habit, then you will be well on your way to daily scripture study. Consider getting up 15 minutes earlier than normal and spend that time reading. Or stay up 15 minutes later at night to read after everyone has gone to bed. If you don't want to wake your spouse, invest in a book light to clip onto your scriptures for reading in bed.

Another great place to read… and this may sound sort of weird… is in the bathroom! Seriously, I keep a set of scriptures in the bathroom and use that time to study. (When you have 6 children underfoot, the bathroom can be one of the few places to escape to for peace and quiet.)

How to Study

Peter explained, "that no prophecy of the scripture is of any private interpretation. For the prophecy came not in old time by the will of man: but holy men of God spake as they were moved by the Holy Ghost." (2 Peter 1:20-21) In other words, the Holy Ghost delivered the scriptures to the prophets and if we are to understand them, then we must seek the Holy Ghost who gave them. Through the power of the Holy Ghost we may know the truth of all things.

Before beginning our search of the scriptures, we should first pray and seek the Spirit of the Lord to help us to understand what we are about to read. We should read with a prayerful spirit and pray for help in understanding during and after our reading. In this manner, we can more fully understand the message that the Lord intends for us to receive.

A particularly effective way to study the scriptures is to write down your thoughts and feelings about what you've read. Even if it's writing no more than a summary, you can gain extra insights as you write down what you've learned and how you can apply it to your own life. Get a little notebook and keep a scripture journal. Or if you prefer typing to handwriting, keep your scripture journal on your computer. Studying with a friend via email is a powerful way to glean extra insights from the scriptures. You can each read the same chapters and then share ideas about what you've read.

For information on our weekly Bible study course, see the resource section at the end of the book.

Why Study?

To understand the importance of daily scripture study, imagine that the love of God – your eternal life – is represented by a beautiful tree with wonderful white delicious fruit and a fountain of living waters amidst a peaceful meadow. In order to reach this meadow and enjoy the fruit and the water, you must follow a straight and narrow path leading to it. Along this path is an iron rod pointing to the tree and the fountain.

Surrounding the path on all sides are dangerous cliffs and precipices. You must travel through mists of darkness, but to help you safely reach the tree, there is a rod of iron to which if you will cling you can safely reach your destination. This iron rod is the Word of God. As long as you cling to it and keep your grip firm, you cannot veer off course. The mists of darkness won't cause you to wander blindly into forbidden paths or plummet to the bottom of the cliffs and pits of life.

Cling to that rod of iron – the Word of God and it will safely guide you to the love of God and to eternal life in His presence.

There is an old Buddhist story about a young man who came to a wise teacher and asked him to teach him all that he knew. The teacher took the prospective student to the river and they both waded out into the water. Then, the teacher took the student and shoved him under the water for an extended period of time, finally releasing the student who by this time was frantically clutching and gasping for air.

After somewhat regaining his breath, the young man exclaimed, "Why in the world did you do that? I came here asking you to teach me and you shoved me under the water until I nearly drowned!"

The wise teacher responded, "When you hunger and thirst for knowledge as you have just hungered and thirsted for air, come back to me and I will teach you."

Jesus promised us, "Blessed are all they who do hunger and thirst after righteousness, for they shall be filled." (Matthew 5:6). When we earnestly desire, ask and seek, the Lord will teach us what He wants us to know and His mysteries will be unfolded to our view. (Luke 8:10) But we have to put in the effort. We have to hunger, thirst, study and apply what we've learned.

Step 4: Faith in Christ

Salvation comes through faith in the Lord Jesus Christ. We are the "children of God by faith in Christ Jesus." (Galatians 3:26).

Who Is This Jesus?

If faith in the Lord Jesus Christ is the foundation upon which we must build our lives, then let us take a few moments to discuss Him and who He is. Who is this Jesus of whom the prophets foretold and whose birth the angels heralded? Who is this Jesus of whom faithful followers have worshiped and revered for thousands of years? How could one solitary individual, of which secular history has recorded but a few lines, make such an impact on the world for thousands of years?

The Son of God

On two separate occasions in the Bible, God the Father witnessed from the heavens declaring, "This is my beloved Son in whom I am well pleased." Once was when He was being baptized by John the Baptist as recorded in Matthew 3:17 and the second time was on the Mount of Transfiguration as documented in Matthew 17:5, Mark 9:7, Luke 9:35, and 2 Peter 1:17. As Peter, an eyewitness to the account, described "For He received from God the Father honor and glory, when there came such a voice to Him from the excellent glory, This is my beloved son, in whom I am well pleased. And this voice which came from heaven we heard, when we were with Him in the holy mount."

The scriptures tell us that "In the mouth of two or three witnesses shall every word be established" (Matthew 18:16, 2

Cor. 13:1). In the mouths of Matthew, Mark, Luke and Peter is the Father's verifying voice established that Jesus is truly the Son of the Most High God.

The Creator

Under the direction of His Father, Jesus created the heavens and the earth. Ephesians 3:9 explains, "And to make all *men* see what *is* the fellowship of the mystery, which from the beginning of the world hath been hid in God, who created all things by Jesus Christ." Again, another witness to this fact is the ancient prophet Isaiah, "Thus saith the LORD, thy redeemer, and He that formed thee from the womb, I am the Lord that maketh all things; that stretcheth forth the heavens alone; that spreadeth abroad the earth by myself." (Isaiah 44:24). And our third witness, John spoke in John 1:1-3, "In the beginning was the Word and the Word was with God, and the Word was God. The same was in the beginning with God. All things were made by Him; and without Him was not any thing made that was made." Jesus Christ, the Son of God, was with God His Father and created everything that has been made.

Our Redeemer

As He told Isaiah, "Thou shalt know that I the LORD *am* thy Savior and thy Redeemer, the mighty One of Jacob." There is no other way or means for us to be saved, only through the atoning blood of Jesus Christ, who came into the world to redeem the world. Paul testified to the Thessalonians, "For God hath not appointed us to wrath, but to obtain salvation by our Lord Jesus Christ." (1 Thessalonians. 5:9) From the days of Adam through Moses and from Moses until the coming of Christ, men offered the firstlings of their flocks as a sacrifice by shedding of blood to signify the coming sacrifice of our Savior Jesus Christ. From the time of Christ on, the sacrificing of animals ceased, but as always, the true token of our covenant remains – that of sacrificing our broken hearts and contrite spirits. (Psalms 34:18, Psalms 51:17).

There are many other titles that may be ascribed to Jesus Christ: Wonderful, Counselor, The mighty God, The everlasting Father, The Prince of Peace (Isaiah 9:6), Savior, the Holy One of Israel. But perhaps most endearing of all is *Friend*.

The Phases of Faith

When I was a small child of 3, my father spent hours working with me teaching me to read. First he taught me the letters of the alphabet and the sounds they made. (He now comments on how laboriously slow this process of teaching me the alphabet seemed; it seemed like it took forever.) Then, as I mastered the sounds, he began to teach me how to blend the sounds to read small words such as *cat, run, ran, bat*. From there the process seemed to catch speed, and soon I was reading longer words from the newspaper such as *congregation*.

I then learned to read small books, and of course longer works as I grew older. Each phase of learning built upon the next. This learning method is very similar to the way the Lord teaches us in life. In Isaiah 28:13 the Lord tells us that His word is to us "precept upon precept...line upon line... here a little and there a little. "

We are admonished to "Trust in the LORD with all thine heart; and lean not unto thine own understanding. In all thy ways acknowledge Him, and He shall direct thy paths." (Proverbs 3:5-6). But this trust does not come overnight. It comes step by step. Just as a child progresses in his ability to read or as a student progresses from kindergarten to elementary to middle to high schools and on to college, we progress in our faith. If we are willing to receive and accept His word, then He is willing to keep teaching and shaping us.

Have you ever stepped out on a leap of faith to do something you felt the Lord guided you to do, but then felt as if you were completely alone? This is a common feeling and it is one that builds faith.

I used to conduct computer training, and at the end of a course, I would give the students an end-of-course project to pursue on their own. Quickly I learned that for this to be a valid evaluation of their abilities, I had to leave the room and let them work on it alone. If I stayed in the room, they would ask me questions, and I would get tugged into helping them more than I should. If I helped them too much, the evaluation was of little value. I always let my students know that I was just in the next room and if they really needed me, they could call and I would come to give them a nudge in the right direction. After finishing this little test, the student's confidence would be stronger and they knew that they were up to real work-world challenges.

Likewise, the Lord often leaves us to ourselves so that He and we can evaluate just how much we have learned. Often these tests come after great spiritual experiences because the Lord is helping us to practically apply the things we have learned.

We must be tested after each burst of enlightenment to see if we will live true and faithful to it. The question to be answered is, "Sure you may have learned these concepts, but do you know how to put them into practice in the real world?"

We move through our spiritual growth in levels, just like a student moving from one grade to the next. Each new level requires sacrifice – the sacrifice of something dear to us. We may not really have to make the sacrifice, but we must be faced with a point where we know we are willing to make the necessary sacrifice.

With this perspective of life, we can take courage when we feel alone that the Lord is really nearby – only a call away. We take comfort in knowing that this is just an evaluation point, and after we endure it well, the Lord will come back into the room to congratulate us on a job well done.

Just as a child must learn her letters before she can read, so must we each start somewhere in our path of faith. The Lord is ever patient. His word for that is *long-suffering*, and thus we must learn to be patient with ourselves. Each trial that we endure patiently with faith and every prayer that is answered builds our faith. When we commit to keep going forward no matter what the costs, God sends us glimpses of hope – not immediate resolution of the problem, but a little packet of sunlight to light our way... and gradually more packets of hope as we continue to walk forward. During my hardest challenges, I've found that the sooner I can give the consequences to Him and do what He asks, the sooner the door opens and the sooner I can receive His loving guiding light. Tough problems are rarely immediately resolved, but they are eventually resolved, and God gives me the strength to bear them.

Jesus promised us a mansion, and in a sense, it is a mansion that we build together with Him. Each evaluation experience adds another row of bricks to our mansion. As those walls start to rise they build walls of trust in the Lord – trust that He will never really forsake us, that He is really always there. We just have moments where He has to pull off the training wheels to let us ride alone to build our own confidence and strength.

From each experience we have with the Lord, if we will remember and recognize His hand, our trust in Him grows. For we learn with each experience that He has carried us through and will carry us through again. As our trust grows, our love for Him grows as well.

As we keep His commandments and reap the blessings of them, we gain a testimony of each principle and commandment that it is for our benefit and our good. We build our faith by doing. John 7: 17 says, "If any man will **do** His will, he shall know of the doctrine, whether it be of God, or whether I speak of myself."

Faith is built through taking steps into the darkness, following through and keeping commandments even when it may seem risky or unpopular to do so, and even when we don't fully understand why. As we take these leaps of faith, we soon discover that God is faithful and is bound to His promises. When we live in accordance with His commands, we learn that His teachings are the one and only way to happiness. With each experience our faith matures.

Chapter 3
Lay Down Your Yoke

Jesus admonished us to take His yoke upon us. What is a yoke? A yoke is a wooden beam that runs across the shoulders of animals or humans to help them carry burdens that otherwise they may be unable to bear. A poorly fitted or rough yoke could chafe the shoulders and neck of the wearer. If it is not properly fitted, a yoke can knock the wearer off balance or cause him or her to tire quickly.

Spencer H. Osborn learned about yokes while traveling in the Philippines. He passed a farmer "carrying an enormous load of vegetables and produce hanging from both ends of a wooden yoke carried across his shoulders." Mr. Osborn stopped to take the farmer's picture and then the man lowered his burden to visit. Osborn said, "I asked my friend if his load wasn't really too heavy to carry a great distance. He replied, 'No, it isn't, because it's balanced.' 'Doesn't that yoke hurt?' I asked. 'At first it did, but I carved and sanded it with a rough stone, and now it fits and is comfortable'"[3]

Step 5: Repentance or Laying Down Your Yoke

All of us carry one type of yoke or another on our backs. This yoke is what we use to deal with life's challenges. The yoke we bear is either one we've made ourselves through time and experience or it is Christ's perfectly fitted and perfectly balanced yoke that makes our burdens light. When Christ told us to take His yoke upon us, He did not mean for us to keep our old, unbalanced and ill-fitted yoke plus add His as well. He meant for us to lay aside our old yoke and take His new and better one upon us. We cannot serve two masters. Either we will hate the one and love the other or we will hold to the one and despise the other. (Matthew 6:24) We cannot keep our old yoke and still wear Christ's.

C.S. Lewis put it this way, "The terrible thing, the almost impossible thing, is to hand over your whole self – all your wishes and precautions – to Christ. But it is far easier than what we are all trying to do instead. For what we are trying to do is to remain what we call 'ourselves,' to keep personal happiness as our great aim in life, and yet at the same time be 'good.' We are all trying to let our mind and heart go their own way – centered on money or pleasure or ambition – and hoping, in spite of this, to behave honestly and chastely and humbly. And that is exactly what Christ warned us you could not do. As He said, a thistle cannot produce figs. If I am a field that contains nothing but grass-seed, I cannot produce wheat. Cutting the grass may keep it short: but I shall still produce grass and no wheat. If I want to produce wheat, the change must go deeper than the surface. I must be ploughed up and re-sown." [4]

How do we plough up and resow? How do we cast off our old yoke so that we can take His yoke upon us – the yoke that is easy and makes our burdens light? This chapter will tell you how.

Acts 3:19 admonishes us "Repent ye therefore, and be converted, that your sins may be blotted out..." As we learn about Jesus Christ and what He expects of us, we are naturally humbled. Humility leads us to repentance. If we come unto Christ, He will show us our weaknesses. We are given these weaknesses that we may be humble; and His grace is sufficient for all those that humble themselves before Him; for if they humble themselves before Jesus Christ, and have faith in Him, then will He make weak things become strong unto them. (2 Corinthians 12:9).

The Analogy of the Onion

When we start out on this earth, we are pure and innocent little children. Jesus often used children as role models. Jesus explains in Matthew 18 that little children are the ones who shall enter the kingdom of heaven, and if we as adults wish to enter there, we must become as our little children – humble and submissive. Whosoever will humble himself/herself as a little child, the same is greatest in the kingdom of heaven. Whoever offends one of these "little ones" – these little children or His humble followers – it would be better for him that a millstone were hanged about his neck and that he were drowned in the depth of the sea.

But over the course of our lives, other people do offend us. Our environment and the poor choices we make start to build up walls that keep us from realizing who we are, and fulfilling our divine mission that we were sent here to perform.

Let's use an analogy here of the layers of an onion. You and Jesus Christ are at the center of the onion. You're there with all your talents, abilities, and potential for greatness that God has given you or ever will give you. But as you were born into this world, your environment and your choices gradually added layers around your soul – layers to the onion, which formed your own burdensome yoke.

How do these layers accumulate? Our first layers are often unwittingly added by our own parents. When a child is born into a family and she is raised, her parents make mistakes. Whether they mean to or not, parents make mistakes – some more than others. The expectations of our parents and their outward directed hopes and dreams for us can often leave a lingering layer that we carry with us through life. It's like packing burdens on our backs. Their poor examples teach us bad habits that later need to be eliminated. Other more malicious parental layers include abuse, neglect, criticism, and false philosophies or ideas. Some layers linger with us and affect us for the rest of our lives until we can recognize and deal with them.

As we start to grow up, go to school, make friends, and become teenagers, we can pick up more bad habits or false ideas that add more layers. These layers can include the following:

- **Insecurities.** Maybe you were the ugly duckling. Maybe you weren't as smart in school and felt dumb, maybe you were made to feel guilty over things that you didn't need to feel guilty over.
- **Vanity.** Concern with vain things of the world – physical vanity, wealth, materialism, popularity.
- **Pride**
- **Dishonesty** – with self or others
- **Immorality**
- **Chemical Dependencies** (alcohol, cigarettes, drugs, etc.)
- **False philosophies, false belief systems**

Our layers are added in two different ways – from our environment and from our own choices. So when you become an adult, you must deal with a combination of both the things that have influenced you environmentally along with the results of your own choices.

Layers can be added in any order and not everyone has the same layers. Some layers are serious sins while others are merely mislaid priorities or motives. If you had good parents and never became enslaved to worldly habits or addictions, your onion could have fewer layers, or at least the ones you

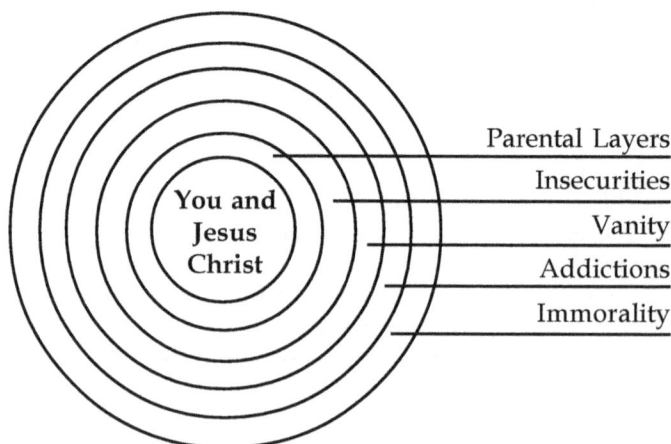

Parental Layers
Insecurities
Vanity
Addictions
Immorality

You and
Jesus
Christ

have might be subtler than your friend with a drug problem. Whatever beliefs, fears, attitudes and habits you develop to help you deal with life's challenges is the yoke you create over time. This yoke often leaves you feeling uncomfortable, fearful, and unbalanced. When you're feeling discontent or hurting in some way, most likely there is a layer in your life that needs to be addressed.

5 Tools for Peeling the Onion (Removing the Yoke)

To get down to who you are – to reach your full God-given potential and have a clean, pure communication with God, you must peel the onion or remove your yoke. Applying and re-applying the following tools can do this.

Tool 1: Humble Prayer

Sincere, heartfelt prayer is the first tool. This is not ordinary ritualistic prayer. This is sincere, heartfelt, broken-hearted, wrestling, crying, pleading and hungering prayer. This kind of prayer is work and it happens when we really have a need, really want answers with all our heart and soul. Many times this type of prayer is prompted when we are at the end of our rope, have hit rock bottom, or have been humbled enough to realize we can't handle a situation on our own and need Divine assistance. Recognizing a layer often induces this kind of prayer. For example, recognizing you are enslaved to an addiction and not knowing how to beat it can cause you to humble yourself in effective, humble prayer.

When we have bad things happen in our lives, it's often God's way of leading us to the point where we will have this kind of prayer that yields results. Think about it, how often do we have this type of sincere heartfelt prayer when everything is going well in our lives? Not very often for most of us.

Patricia Holland explains, "In some sense, prayer may be the hardest work we will ever be engaged in, and perhaps it should be... It is our most pivotal protection against overinvolvement in worldly things and becoming so absorbed with possessions, privileges, honors and status that we no longer desire to undertake the search for our soul."[5]

Tool 2: Scripture Study

Prayer is just the beginning. There reaches a point where simply praying is not enough. We must begin to learn more about the Lord, and the best way to do that is through the words that He has spoken. These are found in the scriptures – in the words of His prophets.

Just as ritualistic prayer was not enough for tool number one, casual scripture reading is not enough here. Studying and feasting upon the Word of God is crucial. In order to uncover our buried talents and gifts and overcome the layers, we must learn more about what God has to teach us about who we are and about our souls. In the scriptures Jesus uses many metaphors for divine influence, such as "living water" (John 4:10) and "the bread of life." (John 6:35).

We eat and we drink to nourish our bodies, but we often forget that our spirits need to be fed as well. Symptoms of spiritual malnutrition include depression, despondency, fear and floundering. When we genuinely study and learn as we read the scriptures, we are feeding our spirits. "Meeting God in scriptures [is] like a divine intravenous feeding."[6] It's like a nutritional injection straight into the center of the onion. Sincere, heart-felt prayer followed by scripture study often leads to the exact answers we needed to hear.

Tool 3: Loving Service

Tool 3 is where things start to get rough. Satan doesn't want us to uncover our soul. He doesn't want us to fulfill or even know what our divine mission is. So as we approach tool 3, he doubles his efforts to stop us, to distract us. He knows that the most important principle of all is coming. He knows that his efforts will be seriously jeopardized if we truly understand and implement Christ's teaching that to find ourselves, we must lose ourselves. So he begins to block our increased efforts to love God, to love our neighbor, and to love ourselves.

As Patricia Holland said, "Remember the great commandment Jesus taught – to love the Lord our God with all our might mind and strength and to love our neighbor as ourselves. I firmly believe that if we did nothing else but faithfully practice love for neighbor, we would have found our ability and success in accomplishing all else." [7]

This is not ordinary love like loving our family members or people who are nice to us, it involves loving everyone – even our enemies. This is an action-oriented love that does more than say, "I love you" but puts those words and feelings into action through selfless service. This type of love only comes when we put the Lord first. It often comes when we freely share the gifts and the talents with which the Lord has blessed us. Grudging or reluctant service does not engender this type of love. But selfless, willing service does.

Sheri Dew said it this way, "How can you tell if someone is converted to Jesus Christ? I believe that the one sure measure of a person's conversion is how he or she treats other people. Almost every major scriptural sermon focuses on the way we treat each other. We are taught to turn the other cheek (Matthew 5:39), to be reconciled to each other (Matthew 5:24), to love our enemies and pray for those who despitefully use us (Matthew 5:44), to serve each other and avoid contention." [8]

With the Savior's help, we must strip away each ineffective layer we've laid throughout our lives. We actually accumulate these layers because we're afraid. Some layers are added in our vain attempts to protect our souls. We numb ourselves from pain or stress with addictive substances, busyness, by seeking worldly pleasures and practices, or by shutting ourselves off from others. But these methods of trying to protect oneself only serve to block the beauty and divinity of the soul that lies at the center of the onion.

What we want to do is learn to trust. This is part of what love does for us. It builds our trust in God and helps us believe that no matter how painful it gets as we peel this onion (peeling onions makes you cry, you know) that it's going to be for our good. We'll discuss more on how to achieve this type of love in a later chapter.

Tool 4: Do All You Can Do

The scriptures tell us to "Remember without ceasing your **work** of faith, and **labor** of love, and **patience** of hope in our Lord Jesus Christ, in the sight of God and our Father" (1 Thessalonians 1:3). "For as the body without the spirit is dead, so faith without works is dead also." (James 2:26) Our ability to hear spiritually is linked to our willingness to work at it and wait patiently for it.

With each layer you peel, the more your trust in the Lord grows. One young woman saw her entire onion, like someone slit it in half, and it totally overwhelmed her. She lamented, "I can't do it, I can't even begin to become who I need to become. There are just too many changes I need to make in my life." It's better to just take one layer at a time. If you want to become a body builder, you don't start off trying to lift 500 pounds. You start small and work your way up. Similarly you don't try to peel your onion in one sitting. You don't try to change your entire life, and overcome all your bad habits at once. You take them one at a time, and as you peel each layer, you get a little more strength to believe that God helped you through it. It may have been painful, but it was worth it. Then a few months later you might discover that you have something else to work on. Because He helped you before, you have more courage to believe that He'll help you again, and it gradually builds your spiritual muscles. Remember the Lord teaches us "line upon line, precept on precept, here a little, there a little." (Isaiah 28:10) It is not necessary for us to run faster than we have strength.

Tool 5: Let Go and Let the Lord Do the Rest

It is common when we have done all we know how to do, that we will still fall short of our goals and dreams. It is at this point we must be willing to let go and let the Lord take over, as He says, "be still and know that I am God" (Psalms 46:10).

There are many occasions in our lives when answers must come in their own due time – in God's time. Often God does not immediately deliver us from financial bondage, from illness, or tough challenges. Sometimes God's delays are a result of our past rejection of Him. Sometimes He delays answers so that He can bring us to a point where we will be humble enough to listen, to repent and to come unto Him with all we have. Sometimes we have to hit rock bottom so that we'll know that there's nowhere to go but up and so we'll know that God is our only hope. Other times, God makes us wait simply to show forth His power through our deliverance or our example – "that the works of God should be made manifest in [us]" (John 9:1-3). Other times God delays or says "no" to our request because it's not the right thing for us to have in our lives at the moment. Perhaps the struggle will strengthen our faith and mold us into the person we need to become. Or perhaps He knows something we do not about the road that lies ahead.

Using the Tools to Peel the Onion

We must humble ourselves, come unto Christ and allow Him to show us our weaknesses and help us overcome them one by one. This is really a lifelong process, but the major layers need to be removed to fully benefit from the remaining steps and to begin identifying one's divine destiny. In order to peel the onion (or lay aside our yoke), we must come to a point where we pay less attention to praise from others so that we are not sidetracked from our path when others disapprove. It's definitely not easy nor popular to peel the onion.

As we begin to implement the five tools, the process of peeling the onion flows like this:

- First we recognize that this layer exists and needs to be removed.
- We become keenly aware of our weaknesses. Our understanding increases, we become humbled and we

begin to develop a "why" for removing the offending
layer. We begin to be motivated to change.

* We gain a desire to remove this bad habit or this false
  belief.
* We commit to change.
* We go through a painful process of removing the layer
  of the onion. Although painful, it is always worth it.
* After the layer is removed, we gain an increased level
  of self-worth and joy. Our love for the Lord increases,
  as does our faith in Him, and our desire to serve others
  and to teach them what we have learned.

Once this layer is removed, we discover new layers that
should be removed and repeat this process as needed throughout our lifetime. Step by step our lives become more joyous.
Bit by bit our faith grows until we know to trust the Lord, to
allow Him to clean up our lives and make them even better.
We learn from experience that He will never allow us to go
through anything that will not make us better in the end. We
learn to go ahead and submit to His will sooner because we
know that it will be much easier if we will and the joy will
come more quickly.

Peeling Clue

The onion analogy gives a wonderful clue to how we should
work on our weaknesses. Think about it. How do you peel an
onion? You start with the top layer – in this analogy the layer
that went on last, then work backward in time through your
weaknesses. For as Jesus said, "the last shall be first and the
first shall be last." (Matthew 20:16).

You'll often find that your deepest and most challenging weaknesses to remove are those that were laid in childhood. Things your parents did or didn't do, or choices that
you made in youth often are the most difficult and tender to
remove. Patience is critical in peeling the onion – give yourself time to overcome your weaknesses. God is patient and
long-suffering and will give you time to heal and change.

In the following four chapters, we'll discuss common onion layers or yoke-bound burdens that many of us carry, and how to remove them.

Chapter 4
Fear: The Root of
Yoke-Fastened Burdens

As women of God, we have unlimited potential for making the world a better place. Women are naturally spiritual beings with great capacity for compassion, charity and service. Women have a power that lasts long after they are gone – the power of influence. Righteous women bring a balancing effect on the workplace and into the lives of those with whom they serve and associate. Righteous mothers have an influence that spans generations.

In a world escalating in depravity and humanistic ideals, the influence of righteous women could turn the tide. Yet, collectively speaking, we are much like Dorothy and her little party in the Wizard of Oz who were put to sleep in a field of poppies just before reaching their final destination. Today a vast army of spiritual giants slumber and sleep. It is as if Satan couldn't get us to join him, so he cons us into burdening our shoulders with ill-fitted yokes full of spiritual poppies. These spiritual poppies lull us away into a dream world where reality fades, nightmares take hold and false fantasies consume our precious lives. These spiritual "poppies" of which I speak include fear, guilt, self-pity, busyness and self-worthlessness.

Fear is the mother of the family of spiritual poppies. It is the root from which the others spring. Fear keeps us from trying, from doing our best, from loving, from giving. We might be afraid of being hurt, being vulnerable, being abandoned, being a failure, or even being a success. Fear is often rooted in very real experiences that we have had sometime in our lives. The things that happen or don't happen to us in

childhood and our youth have a profound impact on the fears
we hold today.

While studying what the scriptures have to say about
fear, I noticed that the words *fear* and *love* are used as ant-
onyms. Particularly, Luke 12 is a rich tutorial in overcoming
fear. What causes fear or worry? Sometimes fear is a valuable
asset. If our children are in danger, then it is proper to have
fight or flight reactions. Mothers have performed superhuman feats and gone to great risks to protect their children in
danger. But often, we let fear rule our lives. Fear is caused
when something that is important to us feels threatened. This
causes us to kick into a fight or flight mode. We'll do anything we can to try to protect what is important to us – no
matter how rational or irrational it may be.

Others can often see the irrationality of our fears, but to
us they are very real and controlling. Often we don't even
know the root of our fears, until we delve down into where
the fear is coming from. Many times, we must dig back into
our childhood to discover the causes of fears that hold us back
today.

One example of this is clearly demonstrated in the life
of a woman I know. Maureen grew up in a home where her
biological father died in a tragic accident. Her mother was
left alone to raise several small children, but soon remarried.
The man she married was an alcoholic. The mother, in order
to dull her own fears and anxiety, turned to prescription drugs.
As a small child, Maureen was traumatized by the loss of her
father and lived in fear of losing her mother as well. She was
so afraid of being abandoned by the key people in her life,
that her nickname in kindergarten was "glue" because she
clung to her mother's skirt everyday when she was dropped
off at school.

When Maureen grew up, she had such an intense need
to belong to someone that she married poorly at the tender
age of 17. She developed addictions to drugs to dull her senses
the way she had seen her parents do. For over twenty years
she stuck with a marriage to a man who wallowed in the same
addictive life-style, crushed her self-esteem with his use of
pornography, refused to support her and her children, re-

sented any ambition she had, and stifled any desires she had to rise above her situation. Her fear of abandonment kept her stuck, until after 10 years of consistently working to free herself from the situation with God's help.

As callous as it may sound, fear occurs when our priorities are out of order. When we put anything in a higher place than God, we block His ability to free us from our burdens and fears. Our priorities may be out of order because no one ever taught us correct principles (as in Maureen's case) or because we have willfully chosen to misalign our priorities. Jesus taught, "For where your treasure is, there will your heart be also." So if your treasure is something that can be stolen by thieves or taken by men or damaged or destroyed, then fear, doubt and worry are going to be a very real part of your life.

Some typical priorities that we often put before God are outlined below.

Family

Families are a divine institution. God instituted marriage in the Garden of Eden. But Christ on several occasions warned us against letting even family stand in our way. In Luke 12:51-53 He explains how His message will divide households. "The father shall be divided against the son, and the son against the father; the mother against the daughter, and the daughter against the mother; the mother in law against her daughter in law, and the daughter in law against her mother in law." The gospel of Jesus Christ can cause divisions within households between those who choose to embrace it and those who reject it.

Being overly concerned with what family members think can cause fear and worry because we will be afraid to progress in our growth in the gospel for fear of alienating them. As Jesus said in Matthew 10:37, "He that loveth father or mother more than me is not worthy of me: and he that loveth son or daughter more than me is not worthy of me."

In Maureen's case, her fear of abandonment from childhood made her cling to family members and eventually her spouse for support in place of God. Each of the people in her life proved incapable of giving her the support and strength that she needed. Only God could help her rise above and conquer her fears, and He did. Although we should cherish our family members and spouse, they must not take such a high place in our estimations that they lead us to defy God and live contrary to His commands. If we do, we will find ourselves selling our souls to satisfy others.

Power

If your treasure is in having positions of power and social standing, these can be lost when someone else comes along who is more popular than you and topples you from your position. Depending upon how bad you want power, you might lie, steal, or cheat to gain those positions. And as Christ said, "There is nothing covered, that shall not be revealed; neither hid, that shall not be known. Whatsoever ye have spoken in darkness shall be heard in the light; and that which ye have spoken in the ear in closets shall be proclaimed upon the housetops." (Luke 12:2-3) Fear of losing power and your desire to do anything for your treasure will eventually cause your demise, because your sins will find you out.

Materialism

If your treasure or love in life is material possessions, then you are building your foundation on something that can be lost. Economies change, industries collapse, thieves and embezzlers can steal. When we are unduly concerned with material things, when they are our love in life, it is natural to experience fear and worry because these things cannot last forever.

Popularity

If you treasure what others think of you, then you are in a precarious position, because no matter how hard we try, we cannot please everyone all of the time. We cannot force people to love us or to care about us. It seems the harder we try to be popular with others, the more we sway and bend until we no longer stand for anything and end up hating ourselves for our lack of integrity. Fear and worry are continual companions to one who worries about what others think of him because this is something we can never fully control.

The Lord gives the following promise and warning about popularity, "Whosoever shall confess me before men, him shall the Son of man also confess before the angels of God. But he that denieth me before men shall be denied before the angels of God." (Luke 12:8-9)

Life

If your treasure is the longevity of your own life, fear and worry are inevitable. Everyone has to die sometime. Undue concern over death and disease can actually cause so much worry and stress that we induce illness upon ourselves. When we spend all our energies focusing on what we don't want, we end up attracting it into our life. As Jesus said, "Be not afraid of them that kill the body, and after that have no more that they can do." The soul's destination is what matters, not the time or method of our mortal end.

Fear, the Antithesis of Love

Fear is misdirected or imperfect love. There is only one love that does not induce fear, as a matter of fact it eradicates fear. It is the love of God, the pure love of Christ. "There is no fear in love; but perfect love casteth out fear: because fear hath torment. He that feareth is not made perfect in love." (1 John 4:18)

As followers of Christ, we should not experience ongoing fear. Sure, we might have a burst of fear in a dangerous situation. This is only normal and is a safety mechanism. But fear that keeps us from progressing in life and from being all that we can be is merely a symptom of priorities that are not in order.

Jesus taught His disciples that life is more than meat and the body is more than raiment. He taught them to consider the lilies of the field and the birds in the sky and how the Lord clothes them and feeds them. How much more the Lord will clothe us if we have faith. He admonished the disciples to have faith, to "be not of a doubtful mind." All these things that the world seeks, the Father already knows that we need. "But rather seek ye the kingdom of God; and all these things shall be added unto you." (Luke 12:22-32).

Jesus said, "Fear not, little flock; for it is your Father's good pleasure to give you the kingdom." (Luke 12:32). God wants to bless us! He is waiting and willing to bless us, but often we tie His hands because we focus on things that don't last.

When we truly put God first and love Him first, the Lord changes our hearts so that we begin to become perfected in love. This love casts out fear. We no longer worry about money or power or prestige or popularity. We no longer care what family or friends may think of us, because we care more about what God thinks of us. The only cure for fear and worry is to put God first. There is no other answer.

Fear, Faith and Opportunities Lost

In Matthew chapter 14, Jesus sent His disciples away on a ship by themselves while He took some time to go into the mountains to pray and rejuvenate after a long day of teaching the multitude. When evening came, He descended from the mountain and observed His disciples on a ship in the midst of the wind-tossed sea. Between 3:00 and 6:00 in the morning (the fourth watch), Jesus went out to them walking on the sea.

When the disciples saw Him, they were afraid and said "It is a spirit." And they cried out with fear. But immediately

Jesus spoke to them, saying, "Be of good cheer; it is I; be not afraid." When Jesus called out, Peter answered, "Lord, if it be thou, bid me come unto thee on the water." And Jesus said, "Come." Peter stepped out of the ship and onto the water to go to Jesus. After only a few steps Peter looked around to see the wind boisterously chopping at the sea, became afraid and began to sink. He cried out, "Lord, save me!" Immediately Jesus stretched forth His hand, caught him and said to him, "O thou of little faith, wherefore didst thou doubt?" They went into the ship and the wind ceased. Those who were in the ship came and worshipped Jesus saying, "Of a truth thou art the Son of God." This account is rich with lessons that we can apply to our lives today.

Many times in our lives, the things that are coming toward us that cause us the most grief and worry are really the best things for us. Just as Jesus coming toward the disciples would bring them peace, knowledge and insight, so our trials and challenges will eventually bring us the same if we choose to look for what can be learned instead of continually crying, "Why me? Why now?" Rather we should ask, "What can I learn from this? What is the Lord trying to teach me from this? What decision will this event cause me to make that I wouldn't have made had not this event occurred? Where is the Lord trying to direct my life?"

We have to make the first move. Often we have to step out of our comfort zone into choppy waters in order to grow spiritually. Jesus was there for Peter, but Peter was the one who had to take that leap of faith from a safe secure ship into the swirling sea. Jesus will never force or compel us. He always beckons, "Come unto me." It is always our choice. We can choose to step out and reap the promised blessings or we can stay in our old, safe way of doing things thereby losing opportunities for amazing spiritual growth.

Keep your eye on the Master. Peter did just fine until he started looking around at what was going on with the wind and the sea. As long as he had his eye on Jesus, he didn't sink. But as soon as he let his earthly environment preoccupy his thoughts, he began to fear. For as soon as Peter began to fear, he lost faith and began to sink. Fear and faith cannot occupy our minds at the same time. We too should keep our eyes on the Master. No matter how scary the surroundings, how bleak the future, or how dangerous and unsupportive our environment may appear, we can walk on the water if we keep our eyes on the Master and have no fear.

Jesus identifies Himself. When the disciples were afraid as Jesus approached the ship on the water, the scriptures tell us that He *straightway* spoke to them to calm them, letting them know that it was He. We too can be comforted if we will call upon the Lord during our trials and challenges. If we listen and watch, the Lord will comfort us even in the midst of trials so that we can know that everything that is happening will work together for our good. We can be calm amidst even the most fear-inducing circumstances.

If we do not hear His comforting voice calling out to us, "Be of good cheer; it is I; be not afraid" it is often because our frantic state does not allow us to see with spiritual eyes or hear with spiritual ears.

Jesus is always there to pull us up. Jesus will never leave us nor forsake us. Just as He was there to lift Peter when He feared and sank, so Jesus will be there to lift us up when we sink with fear.

Fear leads to lost opportunities. Peter was lovingly lifted by the Savior out of the water and carried to the ship, but his fear lost him the opportunity to walk on the water. We do not know whether or not Peter ever had the opportunity to walk on water again, but we do know that he lost this opportunity as a result of taking his eye off the Master. When we fear, take our eyes off Jesus Christ and sink in loss of faith, we can still be lifted by His loving arms, but we do lose precious opportunities – spiritual highs, growth and precious memories that may never come again.

Let us keep our eye on our Lord Jesus Christ and trust His loving arms, never fearing, never doubting so that we can obtain all the rich blessings He has to give us. Keep your eye on the Master and walk on, walk on.

Chapter 5
Self-Pity: Dealing with Adversity

The self-pity poppy is one that lulls us away into focusing on the negative aspects of our lives. The trap of focusing on the negative is that you can't focus on the positive. There is not one of us who has not had bad things happen in our lives. Some may occur because of poor choices, our own disobedience or the disobedience of others, but many times, it's just part of life that bad things happen. No one is immune from the effects of living in a fallen world where disease, death, poverty, natural disasters, disappointment and sin occur.

It sometimes seems that certain people receive more than their fair share of disappointments. One such person is my sister Lisa. Lisa is severely near-sighted, has Crohns Disease, a sponge kidney that perpetually makes kidney stones, has had thyroid cancer, and has lived most of her young adult and adult life in one form of pain or another. Yet, she never complains, she never wallows in it. Instead she keeps her sense of humor, focuses on serving in her church, putting her energy into her home and serving her husband and children. Instead of focusing on all the things she could be sorry for, she uses her energy in positive ways by developing her exceptional art and teaching abilities to enrich the lives of her family and community.

The seductiveness of the self-pity poppy is that it feels so justified most of the time. There's always someone in your life who will tell you "Poor you, you have it so bad! How can you do anything with such horrible things happening in your life?" Listen to this type of self-talk or statements from others long enough, and you begin to believe it. You start to believe, "I can't do this, I'm disabled." Or "If I didn't come from such a poor family, I could have made something of my life." But the truth is, we may not be able to control what happens to us, but we can choose how we will react to it. We can choose to let these things make us bitter or we can use them as stepping stones to become better.

The first question we tend to ask when something bad happens is "Why me? Why now?" Although we can't always know the exact reason, or at least not until some time later, there are some basic reasons why God allows us to endure hardship.

It's a Test

Remember Abraham when he was asked to offer his only son Isaac as a sacrifice? Genesis 22:12-13. Abraham prepared Isaac and placed him on the altar and raised his knife to slay him, when he heard a voice from above saying, "Lay not thine hand upon the lad, neither do thou any thing unto him: for now I know that thou fearest God, seeing thou hast not withheld thy son, thine only son from me. And Abraham lifted up his eyes, and looked, and behold behind him a ram caught in a thicket by his horns: and Abraham went and took the ram, and offered him up for a burnt offering in the stead of his son."

Sometimes the Lord is testing our devotion so that we will know just how far we are willing to go to follow Him. Often, we like Abraham, will be given a "ram in the thicket" at the last minute, but sometimes there is no ram. We must not lose confidence or doubt our faith if no miracle occurs to deliver us. Sometimes the test is simply a test of endurance. Life is a test of faith, a test of our ability to take the long eternal look instead of dwelling on the here and now.

It's Shaping Us

In Malachi 3:3 the Lord says He will "sit as a refiner and purifier of silver." He purges those who follow Him as gold and silver. There are a few interesting facts about the silver purification process. First, the refiner must sit patiently and watch steadily while the refining process takes place. If the silver is allowed to stay in the furnace too long, it will be damaged. Similarly Christ monitors our purification process to ensure that we are not tested more than we are able to bear. A second interesting point about the silver refining process is that the silversmith knows that the purifying process is complete when He can see His own image reflected in the silver. This is the the end result of the Lord's refining process... to mold us and shape us in His image.

Jesus told us to "Be ye therefore perfect even as your Father in Heaven is perfect." In Hebrew, the word used for "perfect" means complete, finished, or mature. Much of this polishing and completeness comes through the refiner's fire.

As C.S. Lewis explained, "Imagine yourself as a living house. God comes in to rebuild that house. At first, perhaps, you can understand what He is doing. He is getting the drains right and stopping the leaks in the roof and so on: you knew that those jobs needed doing and so you are not surprised. But presently He starts knocking the house about in a way that hurts abominably and does not make sense. What on earth is He up to? The explanation is that He is building quite a different house from the one you thought of – throwing out a new wing here, putting on an extra floor there, running up towers, making courtyards. You thought you were going to be made into a decent little cottage: but He is building a palace. He intends to come and live in it Himself." [9]

It Builds Faith

While Jesus was on His way to raise a ruler's daughter from the dead, a woman, who was diseased with an issue of blood for twelve years, came behind Him and touched the hem of His garment. She had said to herself, "If I could just touch His garment, I shall be made whole." When she touched His clothing, Jesus turned around and said to her, "Daughter, be of good comfort; thy faith hath made thee whole." And she was healed that very hour. (Matthew 9:20-22)

When we read this story, we marvel at the faith that this woman had – to only touch Jesus' garment and be healed.

We often marvel at Jesus himself who was so sensitive that He could tell when a portion of His power was being used by another's faith. But something we rarely think about is the life of this woman. She had spent the last twelve years hemorrhaging. And not only would this have been a total aggravation and weakened her into a state of anemia, but also she would have been an outcast from society.

The Law of Moses required a woman with an issue of blood to be separated. Everything she touched or sat on was considered unclean. Anyone she touched or touched her was considered unclean. Even when a woman's "issue of blood" ceased, she would have been considered unclean for 7 more days and then on the 8th day she was to go and make an offering to the priests. (Leviticus 15:19-28). This poor woman had been considered unclean and separated from others for twelve years! Everyone and everything she came in contact with would have been considered unclean.

Can you imagine the heartache and the pain this woman must have experienced for twelve long years? Can you imagine the prayers and the pleading and the cries she must have raised in prayer to her Father in Heaven for healing and comfort? For twelve long years no answer came. No healing occurred. Yet she never lost her faith. If anything her faith appears to have increased with her trial for she knew that all she had to do was touch Jesus' garment and she would be healed.

Did Jesus shun her as unclean? The Law of Moses would have required Him to. But He did not. Instead He recognized her great faith, had compassion on her and healed her according to her faith.

Many times in our lives we must suffer for extended lengths of time – pleading for answers, for relief, for healing. Yet the answer appears to be "No." This does not mean that God does not hear our cries or that He loves us any less. It simply isn't the right time yet. Perhaps we haven't learned all we needed to learn yet. Perhaps our faith has not been molded and shaped to the extent that God knows it should be.

In three short verses, this woman sets a powerful example of enduring in faithfulness through trials that seem to go on and on. She teaches us that we should never blame God or give up hope. Her story is one of hope – that Jesus loves us and that eventually, in God's time, through our faith (whether in this life or the next) we will be healed and the light will come.

It Teaches Us About Ourselves

In the Garden of Eden, the Lord asked Adam where he was. Of course, the Lord who knows everything already knew where Adam was. It was Adam who needed to think about and evaluate where he was (Genesis 3:9). The Lord knows what we are made of. It is we who need to learn our capacity.

After losing his wife, the love of his life, C.S. Lewis wrote, "God has not been trying to experiment upon my faith or love in order to find out their quality. He knew it already. It was I who didn't." [10]

7 Lifelines for Staying Positive Amidst Adversity

The following is an expansion on some thoughts that were shared with me by Vickey Pahnke, a speaker, singer and songwriter. Vickey's friends fondly refer to her as the "poster child for adversity" because of her many health problems over the years. She gave me a list of "lifelines" she uses to help her stay positive amidst adversity

#1 Remember we have a choice of how we react in any given situation

Viktor Frankl, a psychiatrist who suffered years in Nazi concentration camps explained, "Everything can be taken from a man but one thing: the last of the human freedoms — to choose one's attitude in any given set of circumstances, to choose one's own way. And there were always choices to make. . . . Fundamentally . . . any [one] can, even under such circumstances, decide what shall become of him — mentally and spiritually."[11]

We cannot choose many of our circumstances, but we can choose how we will react to them. This is a conscious decision. Our freedom to choose whether to act or simply react is always ours.

#2 Grab hold of the positive

"One thing I absolutely believe in the validity of is actively seeking something spiritual every single day because usually, we wallow in misery. That's a very base, worldly thing to do. The Savior had some miserable conditions but He never wallowed. He always looked up. The symbolism there is looking up – where we're focused. It's all a matter of focus. Some people say to take comfort in the fact that there's always someone worse off than you are. But when you're in the middle of something bad, that doesn't help you. What does help is to figure out something to do for someone else. I believe that no matter what we're going through, it doesn't give us license to treat anybody else poorly."[12]

"The best and most clear indicator that we are progressing spiritually and coming unto Christ is the way we treat other people. Would you consider this idea for a moment – that the way we treat the members of our families, our friends, those with whom we work each day is as important as are some of the more noticeable gospel principles we sometimes emphasize." [13]

#3 Use your resources

What are some resources we have available to us to lean on in our times of trial?

- Family
- Friends
- Scriptures
- Prayer

- Church members
- Ecclesiastical leaders

"This is really hard to do for a lot of us. We're afraid to ask for help for fear of rejection. We have to become as little children to go back home (Matthew 18:3). Little children are not saddled with pride. Little children aren't working an angle. Little children don't have ulterior motives. They have absolute trust in their parents – if their parents are good.

Our quest is to return to that state – to have absolute trust in Heavenly Father, to get rid of the pride, and to see the wonder in the things that really matter, just like the children do. Sometimes it's the refiner's fire that melts all the junk that we don't need on us and in us. "[14]

#4 Really look and listen

"That still small voice is still and it's small so you really have to take time in the midst of all the craziness to really listen to make sure you're hearing so that the Spirit can tell you what you need to help you. Look very carefully, there is more to be seen with our spiritual eyes. Sometimes someone will look at a mother and a daughter and say they look just alike. Another will say 'You don't look a thing like your mother' because people see things differently. Sometimes we see spiritual things, and sometimes we do not. We have to try to use our spiritual eyes.

Here's an example: You frantically look for your keys and can't find them anywhere. Then you take a deep breath, relax and there they are right there within plain sight. That's how it is in our lives. There are means to alleviate our grief right in front of us. But we're so frantic we're not seeing clearly. It's that same principle with all our spirituality. There are things right in front of us, but if we don't have eyes to see it, we'll miss it. Listen with spiritual ears and look with spiritual eyes for the things Heavenly Father would teach you. " [15]

#5 Pray

"James 5:16 says, 'The effectual fervent prayer of a righteous man (or woman) availeth much.' In Luke 11:1 one of Jesus' disciples asked, "Lord teach us to pray." Remember that the Lord did teach us how to pray in the Garden of Gethsemane. That was a very personal communication between Him and His Father. The thing He taught us is, 'Please, please take this off me, but not my will but thine.' He did what His Father needed Him to do. That took an amazing level of faith. None of us will have to endure a Gethsemane, but our own little Gethsemanes seem awfully huge sometimes. There is a difference in saying your prayers and praying. We're talking about really praying here – hungering, thirsting, pleading, and communicating." [16]

#6 Have a Sense of Humor

"When you're going through a hard time, it is wonderful relief and release to be able to laugh. Sometimes I will say, 'Ok, it's time for a funny movie' so that I'll be able to laugh. Children laugh a lot more than adults do – they've studied this statistically. Laughter is good.

Laughter is so important that it's spoken of right off the bat in Genesis. Both Abraham and Sarah, when they found out they were going to have a baby, they both reacted the same way. Genesis 17:17 tells us that 'Abraham fell upon his face and laughed.' Sarah said, 'God hath made me to laugh, so that all that hear will laugh with me' (Genesis 21:6).

The Hebrew translation of the word that has been translated 'to laugh' makes this much clearer so we understand. The Hebrew word which means 'to laugh' means 'to rejoice.' In Hebrew laughing is a synonym for rejoicing. Our laughter should be a rejoicing. That does away with all laughter that is crude, course, is hurtful or is at the expense of someone else. We're adding a rejoicing factor to our lives when we have the kind of humor that would lift us." [17]

#7 Wait

"Just have patience. Sometimes we have to wait. 'To wait on God, no time is lost... wait on.' On His timetable things are answered. There is sometimes a war between our human nature and our divine nature. We need to work on our divine nature because there is a spark of divinity within us. 'We are the children of God' (Romans 8:16). We need to wait patiently on the Lord. "[18]

Waiting is the hard part. The following are two different accounts that express the range of feelings we often experience when waiting on the Lord.

C.S. Lewis said in "A Grief Observed": "Where is God? This is one of the most disquieting symptoms. When you are happy, so happy that you have no sense of needing Him, so happy that you are tempted to feel His claims upon you as an interruption, if you remember yourself and turn to Him with gratitude and praise, you will be – or so it feels – welcomed with open arms. But go to Him when your need is desperate, when all other help is vain, and what do you find? A door slammed in your face, and a sound of bolting and double bolting on the inside. After that, silence. You may as well turn away. The longer you wait, the more emphatic the silence will become. There are no lights in the windows. It might be an empty house. Was it ever inhabited? It seemed so once. And that seeming was as strong as this. What can this mean? Why is He so present a commander in our time of prosperity and so very absent a help in time of trouble?

"You never know how much you really believe anything until its truth or falsehood becomes a matter of life and death to you. It is easy to say you believe a rope to be strong and sound as long as you are merely using it to cord a box. But suppose you had to hang by that rope over a precipice. Wouldn't you then first discover how much you really trusted it? Only a real risk tests the reality of a belief...

Bridge players tell me that there must be some money on the game, or else people won't take it seriously. Apparently it's like that. Your bid – for God or no God, for a good

God or the Cosmic Sadist, for eternal life or nonentity – will not be serious if nothing is staked on it. And you will never discover how serious it was until the stakes are raised horribly high; until you find that you are playing not for counters or for sixpencees but for every penny you have in the world. Nothing less will shake a man – or at any rate a man like me – out of his verbal and his merely notional beliefs. He has to be knocked silly before he comes to his senses...

But of course one must take the 'set to try us' the right way. God has not been trying an experiment upon my faith or love in order to find out their quality. He knew it already. It was I who didn't. In this trial He makes us occupy the dock, the witness box, and the bench all at once. He always knew that my temple was a house of cards. His only way of making me realize the fact was to knock it down....

You can't see anything properly while your eyes are blurred with tears." he wrote as he began his journey out of the darkness of doubt. "You can't in most things get what you want if you want it too desperately: anyway you can't get the best out of it... And so perhaps with God. I have gradually been coming to feel that the door is no longer shut and bolted. Was it my own frantic need that slammed it in my face? The time when there is nothing at all in your soul except a cry for help may be just the time when God can't give it to you: you are like the drowning man who can't be helped because he clutches and grabs. Perhaps your own reiterated cries deafen you to the voice you hoped to hear." [17]

Robert D. Hales after recovering from three major surgeries over a two-year period spoke the following:

"In the past two years, I have waited upon the Lord for mortal lessons to be taught me through periods of physical pain, mental anguish, and pondering. I learned that constant, intense pain is a great consecrating purifier that humbles us and draws us closer to God's Spirit. If we listen and obey, we will be guided by His Spirit and do His will in our daily endeavors.

"Dark moments of depression were quickly dispelled by the light of the gospel as the Spirit brought peace and comfort with assurances that all would be well.

"On a few occasions, I told the Lord that I had surely learned the lessons to be taught and that it wouldn't be necessary for me to endure any more suffering. Such entreaties seemed to be of no avail, for it was made clear to me that this purifying process of testing was to be endured in the Lord's time and in the Lord's own way. It is one thing to teach, 'Thy will be done' (Matt. 26:42). It is another to live it. I also learned that I would not be left alone to meet these trials and tribulations but that guardian angels would attend me. There were some that were near angels in the form of doctors, nurses, and most of all my sweet companion, Mary.

"Though my personal suffering is not to be compared to the Savior's agony in Gethsemane, I gained a better understanding of His Atonement and His suffering. In His time of agony, He asked His Father, 'If it be possible, let this cup pass from me: nevertheless not as I will, but as thou wilt' (Matt. 26:39). His Father in Heaven sent an angel to sustain and comfort Him in His time of need (see Luke 22:43). "[20]

As I said earlier, it does little good to cry, "Why did this have to happen to me? Why now? Why this?" There is really nothing we can do to change the reason why things happen. What we need to do instead is ask ourselves, "What does the Lord want me to learn from this? What does He want me to do next? What would I do or learn now that I wouldn't have had this situation not occurred?" These questions can help us tap into the opportunities that lie within adversity and grow further toward the person the Lord knows we can become.

In summary, as we go through trials and troubles, let us remember their purpose and take the long eternal look toward the rewards of our faith and endurance. This is eloquently summarized in Revelations 7:14-17, "These are they which came out of great tribulation, and have washed their robes, and made them white in the blood of the Lamb. Therefore are they before the throne of God, and serve Him day and night in His temple: and He that sitteth on the throne shall dwell among them. They shall hunger no more, neither thirst any more; neither shall the sun light on them, nor any heat. For the Lamb which is in the midst of the throne shall feed them, and shall lead them unto living fountains of waters: and God shall wipe away all tears from their eyes."

Chapter 6
Accentuate the Positive

Low Self Worth

Low self-worth is a spiritual poppy affecting a vast majority of women today. It attacks in the following ways:

- **Feelings of inferiority** - "Other women can work, raise children, have spotless homes and bake bread, why can't I?"
- **Feelings of inadequacy** - "I have no talents, look at so-and-so, she's just so talented, but I can't do anything."
- **Feelings of worthlessness and hopelessness** - "Nothing I do really matters, so why try?"

The self-worthlessness poppy puts us into a false dream world where we are alone and left to our own limitations and weaknesses. It pits us against our sisters in Christ by enticing us to compare ourselves with others and to place a higher value on another's talents than on our own. It keeps us blind to the vast support that is available to us if only we would ask to see.

The self-worthlessness poppy makes us much like the servant of Elisha. After an enemy came in the middle of the night and surrounded the city with "horses, and chariots, and a great host," the servant arose early and discovered their predicament, he said to Elisha, "Alas, my master! How shall we do?"

Elisha answered, "Fear not: for they that be with us are more than they that be with them. And Elisha prayed, and said, Lord, I pray thee, open his eyes that he may see. And the Lord opened the eyes of the young man; and he saw: and, behold, the mountain was full of horses and chariots of fire round about Elisha." (2 Kings 6:14-17)

We too have angelic hosts ready to come to our aid. George Q. Cannon said, "Now, this is the truth. We humble people, we who feel ourselves sometimes so worthless, so good-for-nothing, we are not so worthless as we think. There is not one of us but what God's love has been expended upon. There is not one of us that He has not cared for and caressed. There is not one of us that He has not desired to save and that He has not devised means to save. There is not one of us that He has not given His angels charge concerning. We may be insignificant and contemptible in our own eyes and in the eyes of others, but the truth remains that we are the children of God and that He has actually given His angels - invisible beings of power and might - charge concerning us, and they watch over us and have us in their keeping."[21]

We truly are the children of God. He is our Heavenly Father. The scriptures are replete with this wonderfully good news. Hebrews 12:9 tells us, "we have had fathers of our flesh which corrected us, and we gave them reverence: shall we not much rather be in subjection unto the Father of spirits, and live?" Acts 17:28 says, "For in Him we live, and move, and have our being; as certain also of your own poets have said, For we are also His offspring." And Romans 8:16, "The Spirit beareth witness with our spirit that we are the children of God."

If we truly believe and understand that we are the children of God, then how can we doubt that He will help us and come to our aid? Why would it matter how much talent or abilities we have or don't have with God on our side? The fact is that we all fall short somewhere. We all need Him to make up the difference. Why must we waste our precious energies focusing on what we lack or what others have instead of building up what we've been given and magnifying it?

Will we be as the slothful servant, who buried his one talent in the ground for fear of losing it, while his fellow servants worked to double their talents from 2 to 4 and 5 to 10? Remember the wrath and displeasure the lord of these servants felt when he learned that his one servant had done nothing with his talent? (Matthew 25)

When we are filled with feelings of worthlessness, doubt, fear and inferiority it stifles our ability to do good. Doubt and faith cannot occupy the mind simultaneously. We limit our potential and ourselves by remaining blind to the hosts of help we have available to us.

Awake and arise as women of God! Go forward in faith. Doubt not; fear not, for when God is on our side, nothing is impossible. Do your best and trust God to make up the rest.

Guilt

Guilt serves its purposes. It helps us know when things are amiss in our lives, when we need some work, and when we've done wrong and need to repent. The Light of Christ serves as our conscience to help us know right from wrong and this valuable compass must not be ignored. With prolonged ignoring of our consciences, they can be dulled until they do not function anymore. Yet, even justified guilt serves a purpose up to only a certain point, and then it becomes destructive.

Women take guilt to a whole new level. Many women feel guilty because they can't be super moms, successful career professionals, glamorous wives with knock-em-dead bodies, and public servants all at the same time. Instead of noticing the good they do, they let the things they can't do immobilize them until they feel guilty most of the time. Unfounded guilt or guilt gone too far manifests itself in the following self-talk.

Unfounded guilt

- I can't keep my house clean and keep up with my work and the kids. I'm just such a bad mother. My husband and children would be better off with someone else.

- Look at so-and-so. She's just so talented, and is such a better mother than I am. I just feel so bad that I'm not as kind and gentle a mother as she.
- I'm fat/ugly/short/tall and therefore am not a good wife. My husband would be better off with another woman.
- I'm not married and don't have children so I can't have as great an influence as my married friends who have children.
- I'm divorced so I'm not as deserving of God's blessings as others who aren't.
- I work outside the home so I'm not as good a mother as I should be.
- I don't work outside the home, so I have no talents or ambition.
- I'm not able to be perfect; I'm just taking up space coming to church. Someone worthier should be here.
- Nothing I do makes a difference, I'm just worthless.

Guilt Gone Too Far

- I'm just no good, nothing I do works. I try, but I just can't control my temper, stop drinking, stop swearing, (or whatever that's being worked on).
- I'm just weak. That's who I am. I'll never be strong enough to change.
- I've tried and I can't do it so forget it. I'm not going to try anymore.

Do any of these sound familiar? I am reminded of another woman I know. We'll call her Tonya. Tonya had a drinking and smoking habit that had lasted for about seven years. It was a social habit in that her husband and friends all joined in either one or both of these activities with her. When she became a devout Christian, Tonya was convicted that God wanted her to remove these habits from her life. But, peer pressure was intense. People didn't let her just say, "I don't feel like drinking tonight." They'd hound her and try to break her will.

After an initial failed attempt at going "cold turkey," Tonya decided she just couldn't do it... at least not yet. Every time she smoked or drank at a party she felt intense guilt. Over a period of 6-8 months, the guilt became so intense that she felt about an inch high. Her self-esteem plummeted. She felt there was nothing she could do right in her life. She agonized, "I can't stop drinking and smoking to save my soul." She felt like a complete and utter failure until one day she decided this guilt was getting her nowhere. She wasn't going to give up hope on overcoming her habits, but she decided this excessive guilt that led to self-pity was beating her down.

What was Tonya doing? She was trying to do it all on her own. She felt that somehow she had to muster all the willpower to overcome her addictions by herself. She had beaten herself down into the depths of humility. In this case, guilt had served its purpose – to bring her to a humble, broken-hearted, contrite place where she was willing to reach out her hand to the only One who could help her – Jesus Christ. Once she decided to stop beating herself up and started praying with conviction that God would help her overcome these habits, He began to work in her life, restructuring her priorities, until she was willing to commit once and for all to lay aside first one addiction, then another. It was a struggle, but with God's help, she beat her addictions one at a time, and her self-worth continued to grow as she did.

"His knowledge of you goes beyond a catalog of your deeds. He knows you individually and completely. He understands your darkest hours when things seem as black as a cave with no light. He understands when you are feeling unworthy or forgotten or depressed or desperate or alone. He constantly and gently invites you to open up those dark recesses of your heart to Him that He may fill them with His light. You can't shock Him. You can't surprise Him. He won't turn away from you in disgust, shaking His head and saying, 'Oh, this is worse than I thought. There's nothing I can do here.' When He healed the sick, He often forgave their sins as well. His healing extends to the crippled heart just as surely as to the crippled leg."[22]

That is the wonderful message of Jesus Christ – that no matter how bad things look, no matter how lost we are, Jesus Christ can help us change. His message is a message of hope. So many times in the scriptures when faith is mentioned, its companions are also mentioned: hope and charity. This is no coincidence for faith in Jesus Christ leads to hope – hope for a better life and hope for a glorious eternity – which leads us to live more like Jesus Christ and not only love others, but to love ourselves.

Criticism

We've already discussed self-criticism and lack of self-worth, but sometimes our criticism is directed outward onto others. Habits such as gossip, faultfinding and pushing someone else down with the false idea that it somehow lifts us up, are symptoms of the Criticism Poppy.

"Why can't we resist the urge to second-guess and evaluate each other? Why do we judge everything from the way we keep house to how many children we do or do not have? Sometimes I wonder if the final judgment will be a breeze compared with what we've put each other through here on earth!...All of this just wears me out because the Spirit cannot dwell in a home, a *church*, or a relationship where there is criticism. Contention neutralizes us spiritually. When we fail to champion one another, we in essence betray each other. "[23]

In John 7:24 we are told to, "Judge not according to the appearance, but judge righteous judgment." This is reminiscent of the Lord's counsel to Samuel when he was called to select the next king of Israel from the sons of Jesse. When a tall strapping son was brought before Samuel as one of the candidates, the Lord told Samuel, "Look not on his countenance, or on the height of his stature; because I have refused him: for the Lord seeth not as a man seeth; for man looketh on the outward appearance, but the Lord looketh on the heart." (1 Samuel 16:7) That day the Lord selected the baby of the family – a young lad who had been out tending the sheep. David wasn't even someone that his father Jesse considered as an option, but the Lord saw David's heart and selected him as the next king of Israel.

We might be able to work to stop gossiping or criticizing, but what about Christ's command to forgive and even love our enemies? (Matthew 5:43-48). What about forgiving and not judging people who have done physical or psychological damage? This is easier said than done when the realities of life set in. How exactly do we love our enemies? How do we forgive and love a serial killer or a child molester or a dictator when many of us have a hard time loving our own mother-in-law? This seems like a very daunting commandment indeed. Most of us just give up and say, "I'll never be able to do that, so why try?"

If love is Christ's greatest message, then wouldn't He have given us clues as to how to accomplish it? Would He command us to do something that is impossible? Perhaps the secret to accomplishing this commandment is hidden in His other teachings.

He also commanded, "Judge not, that ye be not judged." (Matthew 7:1-5). At first glance you might think this commandment is just one more that is impossible to keep. After all, do you let a known serial killer in your front door because you don't want to judge him? Or do you let a known pedophile baby-sit your children? No, you have to use common sense and good judgement. Judgement – now there's that term again – that thing He said not to do.

So how do we resolve this seemingly illogical commandment to "judge not"? Here is the subtle solution. Jesus also reminds us that we cannot remove a mote (or splinter) from our brother's eye when there's a beam in our own eye. First we must remove the beam from our own eye so we can see clearly to cast the splinter out of our brother's eye. What are some beams that we might have in our own eye that would not allow us to remove a splinter from someone else's?

•   How about self pity?
•   What about a chip on our shoulder?

- Are any of us perfect? What about our own sins?
- What about jealousy and envy?
- How about our own hopes and dreams that we transfer onto others – like our spouse or our children?
- What about past life experiences that taint our perception of reality?

It's a simple truth that there is no way for us to know all the facts in a situation and that everyone sees an event from their own unique perspective. So how can we judge people? We can't! Only God sees clearly with no beams. He is the only one who sees the event from all perspectives. We have no right to slap an eternal judgment on someone else, but we may judge things – actions or principles. We do not know the life history or circumstances of the child molester. He may have been abused himself. He may know nothing else. Understanding why he behaves the way he does, does not make it right. Neither does it give you the incentive to have him watch your child. But, when you separate his habit from him, you are then free to forgive him, have pity on him, and yes, even love him. You don't have to love or accept his habit or allow it to infringe upon your life.

When we realize that we don't know all the facts or all the circumstances in another person's life – when we realize we don't know all the steps that led up to making them the person they are, we then know why we are not the ones to sit in judgement on their eternal souls. We may judge their actions. Our judicial system is perfectly valid for determining consequences for actions. But, only God knows the soul, the heart and the mind behind the offending actions.

Yes, we may judge actions. We may use good judgement when we decide whether we want someone else involved in our lives or the lives of those for whom we are accountable. But, when we are able to truly separate the offender from the offending actions, we will be closer to being able to forgive and even love them. Thus, "judge not" is the key to "love one another."

Chapter 7
Choose the Better Part

Women are called upon to fill so many roles in their lives: wives, mothers, homemakers, career women, entrepreneurs, students, teachers, community citizens, home room mothers, and the list goes on. If one word could be used to describe modern women more than any other, I would think "busy" would be the most universal descriptor.

With few exceptions, modern women are busy. Through this busyness something is lost, something of value. Now I'm not advocating indolence. Too much time on one's hands leads to too much self-reflection and too much self-pity which can lead to low self-worth and feelings of inferiority. But there should be some balance in between.

It is this sense of balance that we women usually ever-elusively try to claim. I'm not sure that it is ever completely achievable in mortality, but it is a worthy goal. Most of us turn to self-help books, organizing resources, time management tools, and mini-classes to help us juggle our busy lives. But, shouldn't we turn to the ultimate source of Truth to discover the answers? Surely there ought to be an answer to this modern dilemma. Or is it really so modern? It evidently is timeless.

Remember the account found in Luke 10:38-42 when Jesus goes to eat dinner at Martha's house. Martha was working hard around the house, preparing the meal, while her sister Mary sat at His feet listening to Him speak. But Martha was "cumbered about much serving, and came to him, and said, Lord, dost thou not care that my sister hath left me to serve alone? Bid her therefore that she help me. And Jesus answered and said unto her, Martha, Martha, thou art careful and troubled about many things: But one thing is needful: and Mary hath chosen that good part, which shall not be taken away from her."

What is He saying to Martha? Is He saying, "Stop whining, Martha, you worry too much?" Should we all stop working and cleaning our houses and sit and read our scriptures all day long? No, that's that "all or nothing" mentality we fall into... that it's an "either/or" situation. It is true that work must be done. Earthly cares and needs should be addressed, but not to the exclusion of spiritual nourishment. When all is said and done, the only thing you can take with you is the knowledge and wisdom you gain in this life. It is the only part that "shall not be taken away" from you.

If this is true, and I believe virtually everyone who believes in an afterlife would agree this is true, then why do we spend so little time collecting that which "shall not be taken away" from us? Why do we get caught up in continual busyness and starve our souls? One of my friends says, "If Satan can't make you bad, he'll make you busy." I believe there is truth in that statement. Overall, as a society more violent crimes are committed by men than women. Collectively speaking, by nature women are more spiritual beings. They gravitate to the spiritual much more than their male counterparts do. So if Satan cannot persuade women to do evil, he works to persuade them to be too busy to do the important, to fulfill their divine purpose on this earth. He makes them so busy, they don't even know they have a divine purpose for being here, much less take the time to discover it and fulfill it. Thus, in essence he neutralizes a great force for good on this earth. Righteous women, "are a sleeping giant ready to awake." [24] But Satan does not want us to awake! There is too much we could do to thwart his plans.

Think of the influence that a woman has on society... the typical wife and mother. Not only does she influence other women and men, but also she influences her children and her grandchildren. And if she has done her job well, she impacts the lives of even her great-grandchildren for generations to come. A righteous mother is much like a switchman on a train. Gordon B. Hinckley wrote, "Many years ago, I worked in a Denver railroad office, where I was in charge of the baggage and express traffic carried in passenger trains. One day I received a telephone call from my counterpart on another railroad in Newark, New Jersey, who said that a passenger train had arrived without its baggage car. Three hundred patrons were angry, as well they had a right to be."

"We discovered that the train had been properly made up in Oakland, California, and had subsequently traveled, intact, to Salt Lake City, then to Denver, and on to St. Louis, from which station it was to depart to its destination on the East Coast. But in the St. Louis railroad yard, a switchman had mistakenly moved a piece of steel just three inches. That piece of steel was a switch point, and the baggage car that should have been in Newark was in New Orleans, fourteen hundred miles away."[25]

The destination of future generations lies in the hands of today's mothers, teachers and leaders. Women shape and mold the future. They are the switchmen controlling the switch points that determine what future generations believe and how they act. Yet, most of us go through life with blinders on, like workhorses oblivious to the value of the precious cargo we pull behind us.

Waking Up

The first step to changing behavior is recognizing that there is a problem – awaking that sleeping giant. Some time ago, a friend who used to live on a neighboring farm, but through circumstances beyond her control now lives in the suburbs, was lamenting the loss of her outdoor view. Her son was staying at my house several days a week and when she picked him up; she wistfully longed to have a front porch view like mine and vowed that one day she would again. I reminded her that she was welcome to come by and sit on my front porch anytime. Of course, did I ever sit on my front porch and enjoy the view? Hardly! I was too busy chasing toddlers, studying, writing or building Web communities to make time to relax and enjoy the view 10 steps away from my computer desk.

Then one afternoon she stopped by my house at 4:30 when I was busy at my computer and urged me out onto my front porch to chat, "Come on, come on, get away from that computer for a few minutes and enjoy this porch! It's gorgeous out here!" she coaxed. Reluctantly, I left my email box to join her on the front porch. I had no clue how unseasonably warm it was outside. As we sat and talked, it struck me how blessed we were. We had so much abundance that we didn't even have the time to enjoy it all. As we spoke, I began to see my blessings through new eyes – through the eyes of my friend who could truly appreciate them. Upon watching her drive away, I was left with a sense of gratitude, but also a sense of sadness for my friend who had lost something so precious to her. This was a gentle reminder for me to not only count my blessings but also to take time to enjoy them.

I believe that life is about learning lessons. And one of the biggest lessons we're here to learn is to appreciate what we have, take care of it, and enjoy it. Life has a way of seeing that we do this through three progressive phases: gentle reminders, warning signals and calamity (the whirlwind). It's like your automobile. You know those little stickers that gently remind you when your oil was last changed and when it needs to be changed again? If you ignore that gentle reminder, the warning light will come on in your car. If you ignore the oil light, then get ready for calamity to strike – serious damage to your car.

Our bodies work similarly. Loss of energy or weight gain act as gentle reminders. Excessive colds and flu, low blood sugar, or anemia can act as warning signals. Then, if we ignore our bodies long enough, they'll use serious illnesses to get our attention. Not only does this principle work for our bodies and automobiles, but it also works in every aspect of our lives and even in societies as a whole.

The older I get, the more I realize that I should be listening to the gentle reminders before they get to warning signals and whirlwinds. But this isn't something I'm good at. As a matter of fact, it's a motif for my life – ignore it until it gets to the crisis point then scrounge in a panic to repair the damage. Will I never learn that an ounce of prevention is worth a pound of cure?

As I was thinking about this, I thought to myself, "You know I don't think I had gentle reminders in the past. I think my life went straight to warning signals and whirlwinds." But you know what? I'm convinced there were gentle reminders, but I was just too busy or hard headed to see them. I didn't recognize them for what they were. Over time, I've noticed more gentle reminders and have discovered that they come in many forms:

- My small son peeking around a corner with flirty eyes and coy grin is a reminder of how precious these days in his life are and how blessed I am to have happy, healthy beautiful children. This reminder is saying, "Take time to enjoy them!"
- Seeing my friends and family members struggle with illness or loss, are gentle reminders to appreciate my blessings while I have them.
- A friend pointing out my blessings is a gentle reminder to be grateful for what I have instead of continually running on a treadmill for "more and better" things that I'll just eventually ignore and take for granted too.
- My husband coaxing me out onto the front porch to see a stunning sunset is a gentle reminder to enjoy nature and take time for those I love.
- My weary eyes at the end of the day are a gentle reminder to stop burning the candle at both ends and get more rest.

The list could go on and on. What are your gentle reminders? Take the time to notice them, and then act upon their messages before they progress to warning signals and heaven-forbid, the whirlwind.

This awareness that you've been moving through life with workhorse blinders on and that you've been missing out on the things that really matter is only the beginning. Just because you become aware that you have a problem, does not mean that you know how to correct it or even that you will correct it. It takes time to change old habits, and rarely does that happen overnight unless some life-impacting event comes along to jolt us into line. Such events might be illness, the death of a loved one or a business failure. Sometimes God has to burn our bridges so that we will turn to Him for Him to pick us up and put us back on the track that He intends for our lives.

Sometimes It Takes an Angel

At other times, God sends angels to help us make these course corrections. "Angels?" you might ask. Yes, angels in the form of other people who help us find the way, who snatch us up from the trenches and put us on a higher path. The people who are in our lives are there for a reason, and many times God leads us on seeming detours en route to our goals in order to meet people who can help us reach our ultimate destination.

Too many of us try to muddle through life on our own. We refuse to reach out to others or let others reach out to us. We let ourselves drown in a sea of cares, worries and preoccupations and never grasp the life preserver that is thrown out to save us. I am reminded of a hot Chicago summer in the late 80's. My oldest sister, Karen, her children, my mother and I had driven up from Tennessee to visit my second oldest sister Lisa and her husband. One day we were at a large water park. My sister Karen who is twelve years my senior but nine inches shorter than my 5'10" frame, stood next to me in the wave pool. As a large wave passed us, Karen was caught in an undertow where she stayed for what seemed like forever. Finally, after determining that she had been under way too long, I reached over with my right arm, grabbed her by the scruff of her T-shirt and snatched her up in one effortless swoop.

"Thanks, I thought I was a goner there for a minute!" she exclaimed. "How did you do that? There I was under the water one second and the next I'm flying up into the air!"

We've laughed about that moment several times over the years – about how almost with superhuman strength I was able to swoop her straight out of the water to a standing position without the least bit of stress or strain.

This moment has taken on new meaning for me as I felt one of those arms snatching me from behavior patterns that had engulfed me in a sea of work. For 10 years in business I let the waves of projects, creative ideas and floods of day-to-day business details engulf my life. Ever so subtly, work became my life. There was no "me" apart from my work. I programmed Web sites in my sleep, solved business challenges while I did housework, and talked business with everyone I knew. It consumed me. In 1999, I was reaching serious burnout but when I thought about selling my business a wave of panic hit, "But who would I be if I wasn't this businesswoman? What would I do with myself?"

Now mind you, I was a wife and mother of 5 children at the time, so you'd think I'd know what I'd be doing if I wasn't working. But somehow being a housewife and a doting mother never seemed quite challenging enough for me. "After all" I told myself, "I'd go insane if I didn't have my work." So I plugged along struggling for air amidst a sea of business responsibilities.

In April 1999, I began working with a coach / strategist, Jenette Zubero. Not that I thought I needed a coach, but thought it might be fun to give it a try since many of my clients are coaches and I thought it would be intriguing to learn more about what they do. For the first three months, she helped me streamline my business and create new bells and whistles for my Web sites. I was amazed at what I was able to accomplish with her help.

Then in August of 1999, my life hit one of those points where I felt totally out of balance. I decided to talk to my coach about it. Before this point everything had been business, but this meant delving into my personal life – which I had kept carefully guarded. She began helping me locate the source of this feeling of imbalance. We worked on spending more time with my family, discussed taking my business to a grander level, and set a schedule for finding more balance and relaxation time. Nothing seemed to shake the feeling. Then, finally after reading an article in a church magazine, it hit me what was missing – my spirit was starving. Sure, I went to church every Sunday. I was even actively involved as a leader in the women's organization of my church. I said those prayers that we all say when we're just going through the motions. But I wasn't really thinking about them. I wasn't studying the scriptures as I should. Basically, my work had swallowed up my spiritual life. I was drowning and didn't even know it.

I took a leap of faith and opened up to Jenette about what I had discovered. She was very supportive and started helping me set goals for improving my connection with God. Matter of fact, she encouraged me to share my beliefs with her and in the process of sharing and teaching, I learned things I could have never learned on my own. My faith grew and my life began to transform.

I no longer define myself by my work, by the Web sites I own, by how much traffic they get, or by the revenue they produce. My business and I are no longer the same entity. What freedom to breathe again! I've been snatched, pulled up by the scruff of the neck from the claws of an undertow, into the light of day. My priorities have been rearranged. The interesting thing is that as I began putting God as my number one priority instead of work, my other priorities started to naturally realign. My family floated their way up toward the top of the heap. Now I actually *want* to be a better mother. It's no longer a "should;" it's becoming an increased desire. Now when I ask myself, "Who would I be without my work?" I know the answer and get excited about the response.

As recording artist, Jana Stanfield sings in her *Brave Faith* album, "I believe in this world there is nothing that happens by chance." God puts people into our lives to snatch us from the waves that engulf us. These people who "like a magnet are drawn into our lives"[26] are His angels, His arms to lift us to safety and peace.

Chapter 8
Watch Out for Those Windows

I'm an astronomy buff so I love to watch movies that have anything to do with space and astronauts. In many of the astronaut movies, you'll hear them speak of "making their window." A *window* for an astronaut is a time and a place where conditions are absolutely perfect for them to return to earth. If an astronaut hesitates with indecision, or the craft loses power, or for whatever reason they miss their window, they may have to wait 12 or 24 hours for another window to open. In space 12 to 24 hours can seem like years or even a lifetime when you're low on fuel, power, food or have injuries. Hesitancy at one of these windows could even cost astronauts their lives.

Our own lives have *windows*. These are times when conditions are perfect, when windows of opportunity open for us to move forward in our lives. Our windows of opportunity are like an astronaut's window. They don't stay open forever. They only last so long. You don't have to physically shut your windows of opportunity to miss them; all you need do is hesitate long enough for them to pass.

Let's say you've written a book and have had it published. One afternoon while you are out running errands, the Oprah Show calls. They leave a message on your voice mail saying that they want you to come on the show to talk about your book in an upcoming segment. When you come home and listen to your messages, you're ecstatic. You're so excited and grateful. But then the reality starts to set in. All these thoughts and fears start racing through your mind:

*   I'll have to be on TV in front of a live audience and it will be watched by millions of people! What if I make a fool of myself?

- I'm from a small town. I'll have to fly to the big city of Chicago by myself and I won't know the town or how to get around and that is so scary!
- I'm scared to fly!
- I'd be so excited to meet Oprah, I'd probably just sit there in shock and not be able to say a word.

So, as all these thoughts run through your mind you begin to think to yourself, "Gee, I really need to think about this. This is a big step. I need some time to really acclimate myself to this whole concept of being on national TV!" So you wait three or four days to call them back giving yourself time to think about the idea. When you finally do call, the window has closed. They were in a hurry and when you didn't return their call they assumed you couldn't do it and found another guest for the show. They assured you that when they have another opening they might give you a call.

Now honestly, do you think the Oprah Show is going to call you again? Probably not. And if they do, how many more months or years will you have to wait for that kind of window of opportunity to open again?

There are two spiritual poppies that lull us away into inactivity until we miss important windows of opportunity. These poppies keep us from taking action. These two are procrastination and what I call being a "prayer junkie." To paraphrase James, belief without action is dead. It does little good to know what to do if we aren't willing to take the steps necessary to follow through.

Procrastination

Generally speaking, fear is the root of the procrastination poppy. We might be afraid of failure, afraid of success or afraid that we won't be able to do something perfectly. Sometimes we're simply overwhelmed and don't even know where to start.

Jenette Zubero, a success coach and strategist, gave the following steps to avoid procrastinating an overwhelming task.

1) Specifically name what you want.
2) Specifically name what your obstacles are.
3) Specifically name solutions to your obstacles.
4) Detail how you will implement the solution.
5) Schedule the steps in your planner.

Here's Jenette Zubero's example: "Step number one is to specifically name what you want. Specifically I want to take a hot bath 3 times a week where I can read scriptures and not be interrupted by my husband or children.

Second, name your obstacles. Specifically my obstacles are knowing what to do with my husband and my children while I try to take these baths and have uninterrupted time to read 3 times a week.

The third step is to name solutions. What would be a specific solution for this type of challenge? A solution would be to have my husband take my three children for a walk three times a week for thirty minutes. That would give me 5 minutes to prepare for the bath, and 5 minutes to get out of the bath.

The fourth step is to detail how you will implement the solution. So in other words, I'm going to say that at 5:30 p.m., I will tell my kids that in 10 minutes they are going to go on a walk with their dad and to get their sneakers ready and dressed to go outside. Ten minutes later, I'm going to push them out the door for their walk and prepare my bath.

The fifth and final thing is to schedule it in your planner. It sounds a lot like step number four, but unless you specifically write it down in your planner as something that you're going to do for that day, it will not get done. So schedule it when you want it. You could schedule it Monday, Wednesday and Friday or Tuesday, Thursday, and Saturday. If you want it, write it down in your planner to see that it gets done."[27]

Breaking a Task into Steps

This process works well for anything we are trying to make time for. What about things we don't want to do? We could delegate them to someone else if possible. But if it isn't something you can delegate, then breaking it into small, simple steps that can be accomplished in one work session is best. For example, if you must plan the next homeroom party for your child's first grade class, instead of writing "plan party" on your planner, you could break it into steps and write down

- Make a list of the party items needed.
- Decide which items should be requested from parents and which items will be bought from the class budget.
- Write a letter for the teacher to give to parents about what items they need to send to school and when.
- Go to the store and purchase any items that the parents won't be sending to school.
- Talk with the teacher about any planning needs, etc.
- Follow up with reminder phone calls to parents.

Then, as you plan your days, you can put just one or two tasks on your lists. Only put as many as you can comfortably handle. I like to have all my steps broken down and then underestimate how many I can accomplish in a day. This way, I know I can reach a completion point for the day and feel the reward of accomplishment. And if I actually have time for more steps, then I feel the added bonus of going above and beyond what I had to do.

Tackle the Worst First

If there is a step of a project that is particularly distasteful to you that is keeping you from accomplishing the entire project, force yourself to do the dreaded piece first. Once it is out of the way, you'll feel a sense of freedom to quickly move through the rest of the project.

Reward Yourself

Set mini completion points along the way and then reward yourself when you reach them. It doesn't have to be a big reward. When faced with multiple projects, it helps to tackle the one that is most daunting first, and then reward yourself with one of the more enjoyable projects on your list. Or you could give yourself a break or even a treat of some kind when you reach an intermediate completion point. Reward yourself with something that is enjoyable to you.

In summary, break projects down into steps, decide what your obstacles are and how you will overcome them, schedule your steps, tackle daunting tasks first and reward yourself for mini completion points along the way. Just remember that doing nothing is really a choice, too. If you procrastinate long enough, you can miss important and rewarding opportunities.

Prayer Junkies

Prayer is an indispensable tool in our lives in communicating with the Lord for answers and direction that we need to fulfill His plan for our lives. But there is a tendency for some to believe that prayer is the only thing we need to do, that we just need to pray and rally everyone we know to pray and then sit back and wait for the Lord to show forth His miraculous power.

The story is told of a woman whose business was going under. She decided to pray to win the lottery. So she prayed and prayed that she'd win the lottery to save her business. But the lottery came and went and she didn't win.

After losing her business, she was in danger of losing her home. So she prayed and prayed to win the lottery. But the lottery came and went and she didn't win.

Then she was out on the street with her children, homeless and in the most destitute of circumstances. She prayed and pleaded, "Lord, why didn't you help me win the lottery? I prayed and prayed, but you didn't answer me."

To which the Lord replied with a deep booming voice from heaven, "BUY A TICKET"

I am in no way advocating the lottery or gambling by relating this little joke, but I do believe that many times we are guilty of being like the woman in this story, who was willing to pray, but not willing to do all within her power to make her prayers a reality.

If all I do is pray for my children, but do nothing to teach them, train them or correct them, then what good does it do? If all I do is pray for a poor person down the street but won't go out of my way to feed, clothe or help her, then what good does it do? Does it do more good to make quilts and send them to poor children in Kosovo or to simply pray for them?

James said it this way, "What doth it profit, my brethren, though a man say he hath faith, and have not works? Can faith save him? If a brother or sister be naked, and destitute of daily food, and one of you say unto him, 'Depart in peace, be ye warmed and filled;' notwithstanding ye give them not those things which are needful to the body; what doth it profit? Even so faith, if it hath not works, is dead, being alone." (James 2:14-17). One could also say that prayer, if it hath not works is dead, being alone.

Sometimes prayer is the only answer available to us. Sometimes events and circumstances are out of our control. But more often than not there is something that we can do about the situation. Perhaps the main benefit to prayer is that it helps us see what we can do about the situation. When we do as directed and move all we can in the direction God indicates, we may get stuck again. At this point we pray and get more insight on the situation.

I am reminded of when I worked with a friend who was trying to grow in her ability to keep the commandments of God. We'd work together until it seemed as if we'd hit a brick wall – something that she couldn't find a way to work past. I'd try everything I could to help her, but there would be nothing more I could do. At this point, I would come to the Lord pleading in prayer, "I don't know what else to do to help her see the way. I don't know how to help her get past this. I'm putting this in your hands, please work with her to help her find the solution she needs." Shortly after, a window would open, just enough to let some light through where she could progress and move forward. It would be something she seemingly discovered on her own, or some event in her life that shook her up enough to help her see things a little bit more from God's perspective. He opened her spiritual eyes so she could see.

Then we would work together until we hit another wall. Again, we would plead and pray for help and give the situation to the Lord. Again, another window would open. Through this method of working and praying, my friend was able to gradually move forward in her spiritual growth to overcome some of the habits that had been entrenched in her life as a result of not being raised to know about the gospel of Jesus Christ.

Gordon B. Hinckley has often been known to say, "the only way I know to get anything done is to get on my knees and plead for help and then get on my feet and go to work."

So as we say our prayers, let us ask, "What would you have me do to correct this situation? What would you have me do to improve the lives of my family, my children, my friends? What can I do today to build the kingdom?" Then listen and act more fervently upon the answer.

Chapter 9
Take Up Christ's Yoke

Jesus says that His yoke is easy and His burden is light. In Greek the word *easy* means *kindly*. A kindly yoke, molded and shaped by the Master Carpenter is sanded smooth and does not chafe or cause soar spots. It is perfectly balanced so that it does not knock you off balance. It is perfectly fitted by the Master to form to your exact build – both your spiritual and your physical stature and abilities. But it is our choice to take His yoke upon us. He will not force us to wear it. But the irony is, if we refuse to wear His yoke, then we will wear one of our own inept and clumsy making.

Step 6: Choose to Commit

God will never force us to follow Him. We must use our freedom of choice to choose God. Only we can make the decision to give our whole souls to Him and sacrifice our old life for a new and better one. This requires a leap of faith that many never have the courage to take. Perhaps this is why the Savior referred to it as the "straight and narrow path."

We're often like the young man who came to Christ and asked what he should do to have eternal life. Jesus said that he should keep the commandments and the young man said he had done so since his youth. So Jesus told him, "Go and sell that thou hast and give to the poor, and thou shalt have treasure in heaven and come and follow me." And the young man went away sorrowing for he had great possessions. (Matthew 19:16-22). It's not that Jesus had anything against owning possessions. He picked the one thing that He knew would be most difficult for this man to give up. He required the sacrifice of his most prized treasure before he could come and follow Him. Why is this? Because where your treasure is, there will your heart be also. Anything that has a higher place in our hearts than God blocks our ability to receive the fullness of His blessings. What do you love most in your life? What do you treasure the most? If it came down to God versus that one thing, would you choose God? Are you willing to lay it on the sacrificial altar in order to give your whole soul to Him?

That's quite a sacrifice He asks, isn't it? But until and unless we are willing to seek heavenly treasures over earthly ones, we cannot fully come unto Him and receive the fullness of His blessings. No wonder God is ever patient with us! No wonder He sends people and events into our lives to teach us, mold us, shape us and build our faith until we are ready to give everything we have to follow Him. He knows this transformation is difficult and rarely happens overnight.

In Matthew 23:37 Jesus cried, "O Jerusalem, Jerusalem... how often would I have gathered thy children together, even as a hen gathereth her chickens under her wings and ye would not!" "And ye would not" – what a sad indictment those four words convey. God in His infinite mercy is ready and willing to help us at any time to come unto Him, to shelter us under His protective wing, and give us His ultimate blessings. But it is up to us to choose Him. It is our choice. We are free to choose God now or to take our chances and procrastinate the day of our repentance. It is a surety that the Lord will never send legions of angels to force or compel us. "The Lord wants conversion without intimidation."[28]

"It is only when we yield to the enticings of the Holy Spirit that we can hope to overcome the natural man, who wants to control, is self-indulgent and absorbed, rarely if ever wants what is good for him, and is impatient, egotistical, and demanding. When Jesus said, 'The spirit indeed is willing, but the flesh is weak' (Matthew 26:41), He was doing more than commenting on sleepy disciples.

"Yielding ourselves to the Lord always requires sacrifice, and often a sacrifice of our sins. How many favorite sins are we holding onto that alienate us from the Spirit and keep us from turning our lives over to the Lord? Things such as jealousy, or holding onto a grudge, or being casual about the Sabbath day... or what we watch or read? Imagine the rippling impact on our lives and our families if every one of us determined at this moment to sacrifice something that is dulling our spiritual senses!

"Yielding ourselves to the Lord, from whom we may obtain greater strength than we will ever muster on our own, is the only source of strength in this life and happiness in the life to come. Truly, we must lose our lives to find them." [29]

A mind that is not committed is an open invitation to spiritual weaknesses and sin. "Commit thy works unto the Lord, and thy thoughts shall be established." (Proverbs 16:3) Full and complete commitment to do what the Lord wants us to do is a protection. When we commit to act in the way the Lord wants, our thoughts naturally fall into line and become firm and steadfast in the cause of truth and righteousness. Things that used to tempt us will eventually have no claim upon our souls.

Step 7: Mighty Change of Heart

You might think that forsaking your sins and giving your whole soul to Jesus Christ is the same thing as having a mighty change of heart, but it isn't. The mighty change of heart can only happen when the Savior transforms our hearts, so that we have no more desire to do evil, but to do good continually. Only Christ can change hearts. Not to say that we won't still make mistakes, we will, but we will desire to do better.

Spiritual change is not merely a cosmetic alteration. "The Lord works from the inside out. The world works from the outside in. The world would take people out of the slums. Christ takes the slums out of people, and then they take themselves out of the slums. The world would mold men by changing their environment. Christ changes men, who then change their environment. The world would shape human behavior, but Christ can change human nature." [30]

Perhaps you and I have been inadequate in making changes in the past because we have tried to work from the outside in – we have tried to wait for our environments or circumstances to change so that then it would be easier for us to change. Maybe we have tried to do it on sheer will and haven't leaned enough on the Savior?

True transformations from the natural man do not come by sheer willpower on our part. Although, we have to work to "take ourselves out of the slums." We will not be successful until we allow Christ to take the slums out of us.

Step 8: Obtaining the Pure Love of Christ

Evidence of a mighty change of heart or conversion is the presence of the pure love of Christ in our lives and actions. This pure love of Christ enables us to unconditionally love others even though they may not do what we want them to do, even though they may not believe what we believe or even if they treat us unfairly and cruelly. Showing charity to others is a hallmark of conversion to Jesus Christ.

"None of us need one more person bashing or pointing out where we have failed or fallen short. Most of us are already well aware of the areas in which we are weak. What each of us does need is family, friends, employers, and brothers and sisters who support us, who have the patience to teach us, who believe in us, and who believe we're trying to do the best we can, in spite of our weaknesses. What ever happened to giving each other the benefit of the doubt? What ever happened to hoping that another person would succeed or achieve? What ever happened to rooting for each other?

It should come as no surprise that one of the adversary's tactics in the latter days is stirring up hatred among the children of men. He loves to see us criticize each other, make fun or take advantage of our neighbor's known flaws, and generally pick on each other. "[31]

What is Love or Charity?

Love can be many things to many people, but it may be classified into three basic types.

The first type is expressed in the terms "I will love you if." People give this kind of love if others meet certain requirements. It is conditional and always has strings attached.

Some examples of this type of love include:

- I will love you if you are popular.
- I will love you if you have a nice car.
- I will love you if you attend church.
- I will love you if you are nice to me.
- I will love you if you do your chores, or if you do what I say.

The second type of love uses the word *because* and emphasizes selfish or worldly aspects. It, too, is conditional love. People love others only because of their attractive qualities or characteristics. Some examples of this type of love include:

- I love you because you are handsome.
- I love you because you help me around the house.
- I love you because you buy me nice things.
- I love you because you do things for me, or because you put me first.

Neither of these types of love is true love. They are conditional and based upon our own self-interests.

The third type of love is unselfish and unconditional. We do not have to earn or deserve this kind of love by acting a certain way or having certain qualities. This kind of love can use the phrase "even though." Some examples include the following:

- I love you even though I disagree with what you do.
- I love you even though you have weaknesses and problems.
- I love you even though you made a mistake.
- I love you even though you don't always do exactly what I want.
- I love you even though we believe in different things.

This is the kind of love that Heavenly Father and Jesus Christ give each of us. They love and accept us no matter what we do or who we are. This kind of love is called charity.

Why Is This Love So Important?

Charity is the measuring stick that determines our eternal destiny. Charity is the pure love of Christ, and it endures forever. Whoever is found possessed of it at the last day, will have a place on the right hand of God.

In Matthew 25: 31-45 Jesus taught this truth using the Parable of the Sheep and the Goats.

"When the Son of man shall come in His glory, and all the holy angels with him, then shall He sit upon the throne of His glory: And before Him shall be gathered all nations: and He shall separate them one from another, as a shepherd divideth His sheep from the goats: And He shall set the sheep on His right hand, but the goats on the left.

Then shall the King say unto them on His right hand, Come, ye blessed of my Father, inherit the kingdom prepared for you from the foundation of the world: For I was an hungered, and ye gave me meat: I was thirsty, and ye gave me drink: I was a stranger, and ye took me in: Naked, and ye clothed me: I was sick, and ye visited me: I was in prison, and ye came unto me.

Then shall the righteous answer him, saying, Lord, when saw we thee an hungered, and fed thee? or thirsty, and gave thee drink? When saw we thee a stranger, and took thee in? or naked, and clothed thee? Or when saw we thee sick, or in prison, and came unto thee?

And the King shall answer and say unto them, Verily I say unto you, Inasmuch as ye have done it unto one of the least of these my brethren, ye have done it unto me.

Then shall He say also unto them on the left hand, Depart from me, ye cursed, into everlasting fire, prepared for the devil and his angels: For I was an hungered, and ye gave me no meat: I was thirsty, and ye gave me no drink: I was a stranger, and ye took me not in: naked, and ye clothed me not: sick, and in prison, and ye visited me not.

Then shall they also answer him, saying, Lord, when saw we thee an hungered, or athirst, or a stranger, or naked, or sick, or in prison, and did not minister unto thee?

Then shall He answer them, saying, Verily I say unto you, Inasmuch as ye did it not to one of the least of these, ye did it not to me."

Love for others and demonstrating that love in our actions is clearly a determining factor in measuring conversion.

True charity is a gift of the Spirit. It is not something we can gain only by our own efforts. Charity is a spiritual gift we should seek to develop. Although charity is a gift of the Spirit, and it's rather hard to define exactly how to get it, there are some steps we can take to obtain it. As we work through the 10 steps to conversion, the pure love of Christ will naturally follow. It is a wonderful gift that God bestows upon all those who are truly converted to Him.

We are challenged to move through a process of conversion toward that status and condition called eternal life. This is achieved not just by doing what is right, but by doing it for the right reason–for the pure love of Christ. When we serve others without thought for compensation, acclaim or reward, we express the type of love that Christ has for us.

In *The Bridge Builder*, William Allen Dromgoole describes the typical actions of those who possess this perfect Christ-like love that asks nothing in return.

An old man, going a lone highway,
Came at the evening, cold and gray,
To a chasm vast and deep and wide
The old man crossed in the twilight dim,
The sullen stream had no fear for him;
But he turned when safe on the other side,
And built a bridge to span the tide,
"Old Man", said a fellow pilgrim near,
"You are wasting your strength with building here;
Your journey will end with the ending day,
You never again will pass this way,
You've crossed the chasm deep and wide;
Why build you this bridge at evening tide?"
The builder lifted his old gray head-
"Good friend, in the path I have come", he said,
"There followeth after me today,
A youth whose feet must pass this way;
This chasm that has naught to me
To that fair-haired youth may a pitfall be:

He, too, must cross in the twilight dim -
Good friend, I am building this bridge for him."

The Apostle Paul taught that "charity never faileth." (1 Corinthians 13). The reason charity never fails and the reason charity is greater than even the most significant acts of goodness he cited is that charity, is not an *act* but a *condition* or state of being. Charity is attained through a succession of acts that result in a conversion. Charity is something one becomes.

Selfless Service: The All-Purpose Cure

Many modern spiritualists and self-help experts say that you must put yourself first in order to stop worrying about all the things you "have to do" that you can't. Have a "me first" mentality. This way, they reason, you'll take time to care for yourself and your body, get your needed rest, and have relaxation time, etc. This sounds logical – right? Take care of yourself and you'll have more energy to do all you have to do. But this is so contrary to the average woman's psyche that it rarely works.

Generally speaking, women find their greatest joy in life by knowing that they *made a difference* in someone else's life or in the world around them. So how is putting "me" first, going to help serve that purpose? I guess with some reasoning one could derive the logic, but the average woman is just going to feel guilty and depressed if she goes around with a purely selfish **me first** mentality.

So is there a solution? Yes there is! And it plays right into what women naturally want to do – *make a difference.* Women naturally are inclined to feelings of compassion, warmth and service. When we remember this, and use these gifts, we find the solution to not only living guilt-free, but also a happy, purposeful, and joyous life.

First, the path to happiness and peace of mind does not involve looking out for number one. I find my happiest moments in life when I'm lost in serving and lifting someone else. But the times I'm dwelling on my own problems and challenges and worrying about me, I'm the most miserable. I bet if you think about it, you'll notice the same thing in your life. The irony of this is that we must "lose" ourselves to "find" ourselves. I'm not advocating that we become slaves to other people nor doormats nor that we neglect our bodies & minds – quite the contrary. When we truly live to serve and lift others, we will find sustained happiness, purpose, meaning and we will naturally want to take care of our own bodies and develop our talents.

Here's the logic of the "serve others" mentality: Put your energy into looking for ways to better serve others. Continually look for opportunities to build and lift others using your unique talents and gifts. Build, edify, and strengthen without thought for yourself or what you're going to get out of it. I'm not saying to give away your products/services or your employment for free, but look for ways outside of your work to share your talents and gifts. Or even within your work, do your best to go "above and beyond."

As you do this, and share your talents and abilities generously, they will grow, and your confidence will increase.

As you serve, you'll learn to see the good in everyone – including yourself. You'll learn that everyone has their own unique talents and abilities and their own place to contribute. You'll stop comparing yourself with others. You'll start seeing the positive rather than the negative.

As you see that your talents and abilities can make a positive difference in the world around you, your self-respect will return and you will learn to love yourself again.

Your life will be enriched and given purpose and meaning. You will be happy and find real joy on a consistent basis. Because your life is happy – because "reality" is so great, you will lose the desire to escape from reality through addictions and crutches like alcohol, drugs, food, etc. We get hooked on these things for two reasons

1)   We want to escape from reality because reality is too hard to take.

2)   We aren't finding enough real joy in our lives, so we settle for stimulants that release those enzymes and chemicals in our brain that make us feel like we're ex-

periencing joy and peace of mind. But it's really false. It's just momentary pleasure that is fleeting, so we have to repeat the process until we finally become addicted to something that enslaves us.

When you realize your talents are there for a reason – to edify and to improve the world around you, then logically you know you must nourish your body and your talents. You must maintain a certain energy level and health in order to be able to continue to give and serve so you can continue to experience this level of happiness and joy. You learn to be wise in how you use your time, your energy and your talents. You'll learn that you're only human and that you can only do what you can do. But you'll be making such a significant difference in the world around you that guilt will be virtually eliminated. You'll discover who you really are and why you're here. You'll free yourself from enslaving addictions, and find consistent joy and happiness. Lose yourself in service. It's so simple, yet so powerful. And it works!

The scriptures teach us to tithe. And many of us do that monetarily by paying 10 percent of our income to the Lord. This is wonderful, but I would suggest going above and beyond. If you really want to reach the next spiritual level, tithe your time, talents and abilities. Each day think of ways you can use your time, talents and abilities that the Lord has blessed you with and share them with others.

Malachi 3:10's promises "Bring ye all the tithes into the storehouse, that there may be meat in mine house, and prove me now herewith, saith the Lord of hosts, if I will not open you the windows of heaven, and pour you out a blessing, that there shall not be room enough to receive it."

I testify to you that nothing can compare to the increased self-confidence, self worth, and sheer joy that comes when we not only tithe in a monetary way, but also tithe our time, talents and abilities and consecrate them to the Lord to bless others. Truly, "the windows of heaven" will be opened to you and the Lord will, "pour you out a blessing, that there shall not be room enough to receive it."

Chapter 10
Discover Your Mission

Step 9: Catch the Vision

N
o woman is more persuasive, no woman has greater influence for good, no woman is a more vibrant in strument in the hands of the Lord than a woman of God who is thrilled to be who she is." [32]

As we receive Christ's mighty change in our hearts, we begin to be filled with His love which motivates us to use our God-given talents and abilities to selflessly serve others. As we do this, we will catch the vision of who we are and why God has placed us here on this earth at this time and in the lives of those with whom we come in contact. The closer we get to Jesus Christ, the clearer our vision of ourselves and what we can ultimately achieve and become. We might call it an *eye of faith*.

Sheri Dew explained it this way, "Yes, life *is* a test—of many things. But at the risk of sounding simplistic, may I suggest that the mortal experience is largely about vision—our vision of ourselves and our ultimate Big Finish. And vision is determined by faith. The firmer our faith in Jesus Christ, the clearer our vision of ourselves and what we can ultimately achieve and become.

The adversary, of course, is intent on obstructing our vision and undermining our faith. He will do anything and everything to confuse us about who we are and where we're going because he has already forfeited his privilege of going there. A vision of our potential is central to survival—both spiritually and physically." [33]

Once you have shed your own awkward, ill-fitted yoke and have taken on Christ's kindly yoke, you are free and unburdened. The beauty of your soul could be compared to the beauty of a temple. As Paul said, "Know ye not that ye are the temple of God?" (1 Corinthians 3:16).

You are holy – the divinity is abiding within you waiting to be uncovered – to be unleashed and magnified and demonstrated. The purpose of your existence is to be an instrument in His hands, to be joint heirs with Christ. As Psalms 82:6 says, "I have said, 'Ye are gods; and all of you are children of the most High.'" Jesus also taught this in John 10:34, "Is it not written in your law, 'I said, Ye are gods?'" We are made in our Father's image and our destiny is to share in His glory – to become "joint heirs with Christ" (Romans 8:17).

Any woman who wishes to find her true identity and value as a daughter of God and become the influence that God knows she can be must make this journey of conversion, which in the end leads to her soul. Then, and only then, will she become the phenomenal influence for good that is locked within her.

As you progress through the steps of the conversion process, inklings and foretastes of your mission begin to appear. Your mission will become inescapable. You won't be able to avoid being compelled from within to fulfill the mission that is yours. You will want it with everything you have and are. There will be no denying it.

Evaluate the Building Blocks of Your Mission

Isaiah 51:1 gives the ingredients for being a righteous servant of the Lord, "Hearken to me, ye that follow after righteousness, ye that seek the Lord: look unto the rock whence ye are hewn, and to the hole of the pit whence ye are digged." When you are trying to understand your mission, you'll want to look to two important places -- the rock from whence you were hewn and the hole of the pit from whence you were dug. What does this mean?

As is common with Isaiah, there are multiple meanings for this recommendation. In the verse that follows, Isaiah talks about Abraham and Sarah, "Look unto Abraham your father, and unto Sarah that bare you: for I called him alone, and blessed him, and increased him." One interpretation of this passage is that Isaiah is telling the children of Israel to look to Abraham and Sarah (their ancestors). Abraham and Sarah set a powerful example of devotion, dedication, commitment, covenant-keeping and a willingness to sacrifice everything to serve the Lord. The Lord blessed them accordingly.

We too can look to Abraham and Sarah as examples. When we make and keep covenants with the Lord, we are also heirs to the same blessings that Abraham was promised. But, a second interpretation for Isaiah 51:1 yields even greater insights into the process of discovering your divine destiny.

The Rock Whence Ye Were Hewn

In this second interpretation, the rock whence ye were hewn is what you are made of - who you are. You are a child of God, hewn from The Rock - God Himself. You have spiritual gifts which you inherited from Him. In addition, you have unique talents, characteristics, interests, and abilities. This is the rock from whence you are hewn. So when trying to understand your divine destiny, it is important to evaluate your interests and talents.

Take a Talent Inventory

- What do people tell you that you do well? What kind of compliments do you receive from others now or in the past?
- What kind of activities do you enjoy?
- Do you relate better to children, youth, adults, the elderly, animals?
- What is your preferred method of communicating? On the phone? Email? Writing? Speaking? Teaching?
- Do you enjoy helping a friend with her problems?
- Do you enjoy music? In what ways: listening, playing, performing, leading, writing?
- Do you enjoy the arts? What types: painting, drawing, crafts, quilting, sewing, decorating, photography, scrapbooking etc?

- Do you enjoy gardening, growing flowers, plants, or vegetables?
- Do you enjoy cooking?
- Do you enjoy cleaning and organizing?
- Do you enjoy reading?
- What else do you enjoy?

Combine your interests. For example, let's suppose you enjoy visiting with friends, quilting, and reading. You might gather with a group of women each week or each month and work on quilts and discuss uplifting books that you read with them. In this way you can uplift and inspire others while sharing and developing your God-given talents and abilities.

Or maybe you enjoy young people, creating crafts and painting. You might volunteer to work with youth groups, teaching them how to make crafts or how to paint. In this way you are building and developing your own talent while helping youth do something positive and uplifting as well as helping them develop their own talents.

The Hole of the Pit Whence Ye Were Digged

What challenges or trials have you endured and overcome? What lessons have you learned through the school of hard knocks? This is the hole of the pit from whence you were dug. God doesn't want you to berate yourself for past mistakes for which He has forgiven you; neither does He wish you to be bitter or feel He loves you any less because of the hardships you've endured. He wants you to remember how He delivered you. He wants you to remember what you were before He transformed you. Remembering this will keep you grateful and better able to serve others.

God never wastes the pain. When you turn your life over to Him, He can make all your mistakes, poor choices, and unfortunate circumstances work together for your good, and usually for the good of others. Countless individuals are able to, with God's help, overcome difficult trials such as lawsuits, divorce, addictions, and abuse and then use those experiences to better understand and help others who are enduring similar circumstances.

Even though you may feel alone in your challenges, there is no temptation or challenge which is not common to others (1 Corinthians 10:13). The trials that you endure and the lessons you learn in overcoming them build valuable character traits and knowledge that you can use to serve others going through similar troubles.

So, your mission will involve using your life experiences combined with your unique talents and interests as an instrument in God's hands to selflessly serve others. It's that simple. He gave you everything you need to accomplish your mission. It's what you are ideally suited to do.

Be prayerful. Ask the Lord to help you catch a vision of your mission. Prayerfully consider the following questions. What do you like to do and with whom do you like to spend your time? What lessons have you learned from your journey through life? Combine these three in as many ways as you can think of and then prayerfully select the most appealing combination with which to start.

Here's an example. Let's say you have overcome addictions in your life, enjoy the goal-setting process and working with youth. You could combine these experiences and interests by volunteering as a youth mentor: helping youth to set and achieve worthy goals and to stay away from drugs.

Another example, let's say you once were overweight, but have learned to adapt your eating and exercise habits to be healthier and maintain an ideal weight. If you also enjoy the company of other women, you might start a support group for women where you study healthy eating habits, hold each other accountable, and exercise together.

Enjoy yourself! Heavenly Father created you that you might have joy, and joy is to be found in service. He gave you your innate talents, abilities and interests so that you could build your self worth while serving and edifying others. He never wastes the road you've traveled.

As you progress through the steps of the conversion process, your mission will become clearer and clearer to you. Pray and ask the Lord to bring clarity and vision. As this clarity comes, line upon line, your mission will become a compelling force that you will have no desire to avoid. As your purpose starts to take shape, it helps to write down your thoughts and feeling and organize them into a succinct mission statement that can focus and govern your actions. The following is an exercise you can use to help you develop your mission statement.

Define Your Mission

Prayerfully complete the following exercise while keeping in mind what we've discussed about your life experiences, talents and interests.

1. *Create mini mission statements for each area of your life: (give some thought & time to developing these)* For each area listed below, write down the characteristics of the person you would like to be. Describe the "perfect you" in each area of your life. Use only positive attributes and characteristics. For example, instead of saying, "never scream at my kids" you could say "always respond to others with patience, love and consistency."

Daughter of God
Friend
Wife
Mother
Career/Business Person
Citizen

Other roles you fulfill might include: Grandparent, Sunday School Teacher, Physical Development, Athlete, etc.

2. *Next, create a summary mission statement based on the contents and similarities of the mini mission statements.* Now you should have completed a paragraph or two under each area. Go back and reread your statements for each of these areas. Look for the similarities and common characteristics found among them

all. For example, under your *Mother* heading it may say "give the necessary time and attention to my children." Under business you may have "listen to the needs of my customers with respect and a desire to serve them." Both deal with other people and giving them the necessary respect, attention and sincere listening. So, your summary mission statement would include something like this, "Always listen to others with respect and attention and a desire to serve their needs."

Compose a summary mission statement by analyzing your mini-mission statements for commonalties. Some areas may contain statements that do not cross into other areas. Write these in a broad way in your summary statement so that it can be applicable to other areas of your life.

Once you have all the ideas in your summary mission statement, read over it. Take time to polish it. Rewrite it if necessary until it means something to you and can be a part of your life.

3. *Now, write your statement on a 3x5 card and put it somewhere you will look daily or even twice a day.* You could use your 3x5 card as a bookmark for your scriptures so that you will be sure to read it every day. Work on memorizing it. Then, when an opportunity develops, run through your mission statement in your mind to see if it is compatible. If it is incompatible with your mission statement, do not do it.

It is amazing how quickly this mission statement becomes a part of you. You will not immediately change your actions and become the person on the card, but you will catch yourself when you are doing something contrary to your mission statement. Your mission statement will direct your actions and the goals you set. It also helps eliminate many last minute decisions. Be patient. No one changes overnight. It took time to develop your current habits and characteristics, and it will take time to change them. Yet, it is amazing how a few weeks of reading this statement daily will lead you, almost subconsciously, toward opportunities that fulfill your mission.

Chapter 11
Live Your Destiny

Step 10: Remember & Endure

It had been at least a year since I sat down at the battered, out-of-tune piano that occupies my livingroom. It's the same piano I practiced through thirteen years of piano lessons – from the time I was 5 until I broke my arm in an auto accident at age 17.

Sitting in front of the chipped ivory keys was like sitting down to chat with an old friend who lets you pick up exactly where you left off years earlier. Opening a songbook, I selected one of my favorite songs. Much to my astonishment, my fingers still remembered the notes, and I was able to play a somewhat complicated piece without too many mistakes. Some things you never forget, I suspect.

Seconds barely passed before four little hands joined me. I'm positive my three-year-old daughter and one-year-old son were convinced that their accompaniment enhanced the melody to new heights. I couldn't help remembering my grandmother who let me strike the upper octave notes as she played *Red Wing*. At the age of four or five, I believed my contribution added such grandeur to the piece. Maybe that's because her praise and encouragement made me believe that it did. I realize now, of course, that all it really amounted to was a bunch of noise.

Song after song they pounded and sang along. Normally, this would have been extremely distracting, but I found that if I concentrated on the melody, I could tune out all the noise around me. I didn't notice their banging, their singing or even the TV in the next room. The melody went straight to my heart as I concentrated on the words of the song I played:

"I feel my Savior's love in all the world around me. His Spirit warms my soul through everything I see. He knows I will follow Him, Give all my life to Him. I feel my Savior's love – the love He freely gives me."[34]

Anyone else entering the room would have thought it was the biggest bunch of noise they'd ever heard. But as I played and thought about the words, I felt the message of the song so intensely. It didn't matter that chaos surrounded me, the message and melody dominated my thoughts.

As I played it struck me that this is like our lives. The clutter and clamor of daily living can so easily drown out the Savior's love and His message if we let it. The only way we can stay trained on the melody and the message is by carefully listening for it and actively participating in the melody. Being a contributor to the melody makes it so much easier to distinguish it from all the distractions and busyness of life. Discovering and fulfilling our compelling mission helps us remember to listen for the melody. But even then, we humans have a terrible tendency to forget.

It is so easy for us to forget the greatness of God. Moses continually told the Israelites to remember their bondage in Egypt and the Lord's deliverance. He said, "Remember this day, in which ye came out from Egypt, out of the house of bondage; for by strength of hand the LORD brought you out from this place." (Exodus 13:3). Why do you think it is so important to remember our past challenges and the Lord's deliverance from them? Judges 8:34 says, "And the children of Israel **remembered not** the LORD their God, who had delivered them out of the hands of all their enemies on every side, and **they fell into iniquity**."

"As our testimony of God the Father and His Son Jesus Christ expands and matures, our view of ourselves and our potential does likewise, and we begin to focus more on life forever than life today. But when we forget our Father and His Son, we forget who we are, and almost inevitably our behavior disappoints us." [35]

How can we remember? It is the small and simple things that help us stay on track. Attending church, daily scripture study, daily prayers, and making and keeping covenants with the Lord all help us remember Him and what He's done for us.

Inspirational music can help us remember the Lord and his blessings. In the Old Testament, Moses set the historical events of the Israelites' deliverance to music (Exodus 15). Moses knew that music touches the soul on a profoundly emotional level and that it would help the people remember the Lord and their deliverance. Make sure the music you listen to is clean and inspiring. Collect music that will uplift your soul when you are struggling and help you remember all that God has done for you.

Another tool in remembering is keeping a written record of your spiritual progress. A journal or even emails to a confidant can be used as a history of your spiritual progress. Refer to these written records often to help you remember what the Lord has done and is doing in your life.

Consider keeping a daily spiritual journal of the things you learn. As you read your scriptures, jot down notes of how what you have read applies to you. Write down the things for which you are praying, and document when those prayers are answered. Over time, you will collect a marvelous written record of the evidence of God's workings in your life. You will be able to see how He shaped and molded your life. You'll become adept at recognizing when the Lord is trying to steer you in a new direction, helping you to develop a new talent or introducing you to someone you can serve or who will teach you valuable lessons. Without a written record, it is so easy to forget all the times that the Lord has blessed you. But with it, you will find courage when you are afraid and strength to continue when you are weak. You will know with a surety that all things do indeed work together for your good because you love Him and are called to fill a divine mission. (Romans 8:28).

Ask for Opportunities to Serve

As we share what we learn with others, we remember where we've been and how far the Lord has brought us. Make it a daily part of your morning prayers to ask the Lord for ways that you can serve others and help to build His kingdom. In his little book, *The Prayer of Jabez*, Bruce Wilkinson uses the lesser-known Biblical hero, Jabez's prayer to illustrate how Jabez became "more honorable than his brethren." The prayer is found in 1 Chronicles 4:10, "And Jabez called on the God of Israel, saying, Oh that thou wouldest bless me indeed, and enlarge my coast, and that thine hand might be with me, and that thou wouldest keep *me* from evil, that it may not grieve me! And God granted him that which he requested."

The four elements of Jabez' prayer were:

1)   He asked the Lord to bless him.
2)   He asked the Lord to enlarge his coast, or in other words, enlarge his opportunities to influence and serve. He asked the Lord to make him more than he was before.
3)   He asked for the Lord's hand to be with him. In other words, he asked for the Lord's help and guidance and for His Spirit to be with him so he could handle the opportunities that flowed.
4)   He asked to be kept from evil. He asked for help in avoiding and sidestepping temptation. He didn't ask the Lord to help him *through* temptation, he asked the Lord to help him *stay away* from it completely.

The prayer of Jabez is a perfect model to help us remember the Lord and to remember who we are, our importance to Him, and our divine destiny. By incorporating these elements into our daily prayers, we can't help but remember because

1)   We will be asking for the Lord's blessings.
2)   We will be asking each day that He give us opportunities to use our time, talents and abilities to serve Him and build His Kingdom.
3)   We will be asking for His Spirit to be with us, or His "hand to be with us." In order to expect to have His Spirit to be with us, we know that we must remember Him and be living in a manner that pleases Him. Hav-

ing His hand with us is critical when we have asked for opportunities to serve, because the opportunities that come are usually bigger than what we can handle on our own.

4) We will be consistently asking for help in sidestepping temptation and being kept from the evil influences of the world around us.

This formula works. I actually stumbled upon this combination a year or so before reading *The Prayer of Jabez*. All my life, I've been taught to pray to have His Spirit with me, to be able to keep His commandments, and to ask for His blessings. But not until a year or so ago did I actively start praying for the Lord to send me opportunities to serve Him. When I started praying for the Lord to send me people I could help and when I started letting Him know that I really wanted to be a part of building His Kingdom, I was amazed at the results. People started coming to me from everywhere. I could spend an entire day answering emails and teaching others what I'd learned. It was like a flood of opportunities and blessings poured out on my head.

A Warning

I must add a bit of a warning here. Don't make my mistake. The flood of people coming to me began to be a little bit overwhelming. I was extremely blessed in this, maybe I was too blessed? My home business grew by 50% even though I spent only a fraction of the time I used to spend on it and my family relationships improved. I think it became a little emotionally overwhelming to have so many people asking my advice, leaning on me for support or asking me to tell them about the gospel. It seemed bigger than I was, and it really was. But I knew that if I had the Spirit with me, I could handle it.

I'm not sure why, but I think it had to do with my business growth and learning that I was expecting my sixth baby that made me slow down the pace. I gradually began only asking the Lord to send me opportunities on the days that I didn't have a lot of other work to do. My logic was, "I've got some things of my own I need to do today, I'll just say a regular prayer today and not ask for the extra opportunities, because I don't have time for that today."

Some days I did better. I prayed, "Heavenly Father, help me accomplish this and that and then I'd be happy to use the rest of my time on whatever you need me to do." That worked. He always helped me accomplish what I needed to and still left time to do what He wanted me to do. I'm not sure why or when I stopped asking for the opportunities to serve above and beyond. Eventually, I reduced my asking to maybe once or twice a week. Then because I had fewer people's problems and challenges to research, I began reducing the time I spent really studying the scriptures like I should, and accordingly the opportunities diminished.

When I didn't ask, I didn't receive. What I learned from this is that *we control the flow of the Lord's opportunities and blessings*. We can run as fast as we want to. If we decide to slow down and walk, the Lord will let us slow down and walk. But nothing beats the exhilaration and the sheer joy of running with the wind. When we refuse to run, we miss out on abundant blessings.

The greatest danger in slowing down our pace is that it is so extremely easy to forget what it felt like to run. We get out of shape spiritually, and it becomes so much more difficult to remember how to run again. We become lazy and slothful and lax in our scripture study and prayers. It's so easy to slip back to where you started without constant vigilance.

As I desired to pick up the pace, I asked the Lord to help me set a pace that I could physically and emotionally handle – one that is suited to my time, abilities and family's needs. All things must be done in wisdom and in order. The Lord does not require us to run faster than we have strength. What is important is that we are diligently moving forward toward the prize. That diligence comes from continually studying our scriptures on a daily basis, offering consistent fervent prayers, and looking for opportunities to serve where we are able. Whatever you do, don't slacken your scripture study or prayers just to slow things down. Ask the Lord to give you what you can handle while hanging onto the lifelines of scriptures, journal keeping and prayer. Letting go is too dangerous because remembering becomes so difficult without them.

If you fail to remember and endure, you will start sliding back down the steps. The steps work in reverse too. If you fail to remember and endure, you'll start to lose your vision. If you lose your vision, you'll have a tougher time loving others with the pure love of Christ. If you slip further, you'll lose your change of heart and you'll lay aside Christ's yoke and take up your old one that you used to wear.

If you start having a tougher time loving others or if you start feeling discontent, depressed or that something is amiss, start remembering and enduring. Repent where necessary. Pull out your journal and recall how you used to be and how the Lord delivered you. Review your mission statement daily. Start praying earnestly for clarity of vision and immerse yourself in the Word of God. Remembering and enduring is critical. It's your maintenance plan that keeps you moving forward on the strait and narrow path toward your goal.

Conclusion

It is much easier to remember and endure if you have clarity of vision. Rarely do we receive one overwhelming manifestation of our future that continually propels us forward. Rather, most of us are given information about our mission on a need-to-know basis. God gives us a piece at a time until the puzzle starts to form a distinct picture. Seek out your vision. Work for it, pray for it, keep going through these steps until you receive it.

Don't stop there. Keep following in the shadow of the Master. Conversion isn't a onetime event. It's a lifelong process of being and becoming like Jesus Christ, our great Exemplar. Forsaking our old ways and following the Savior is the greatest thing we can do with our lives. Come unto Christ. Give your whole soul to Him. For then and only then will you find happiness, joy and peace in this life and the next.

My prayer is that every person reading this book will come to not only believe in Jesus Christ, but also believe Him when He says He can wash away your sins, bind up your broken heart and transform your life. May you know from experience the wonderful transforming power of the Savior and know with every fiber of your being that He lives and loves you. May you be filled with His pure love that gives you no more desire to do evil, but to do good continually, and to love your neighbor as yourself. May you commit and say, "I will give away all my sins to know Thee. Whatever the consequences, I want to do what's right. I *want* to follow Thee." It is only after we wholeheartedly choose and commit to follow Him that Christ can work His mighty miracle in our hearts.

Although I have never seen Him, I leave my testimony with you that I know that He lives for I have experienced His transforming influence in my life. I have tasted of the sweetness of His love. He loves you and wants you to be happy. He wants you to live a fulfilled and abundant life and then return to live with Him again. It's all yours for the choosing. *Remember, you control the flow of His blessings!*

Bibliography

1 Boyd K. Packer, "Reverence Invites Revelation," *Ensign*, Nov. 1991, p. 21-22

2 Sheri L. Dew, *"As Women of God, Shall We Not Go Forward In So Great a Cause,"* BYU Women's Conference 2000

3 Spencer H. Osborn, "Service in the Church," *Ensign*, November 1984, 76

4 C.S. Lewis, *Mere Christianity*, p 170

5 Patricia Holland, *Many Things...One Thing*, The Best of Women's Conference, BookCraft 2000,p. 197.

6 Patricia T. Holland, *Many Things...One Thing*, The Best of Women's Conference, BookCraft 2000, p 198.

7 Ibid.

8 Derived from Sheri L. Dew, *As Women of God, Shall We Not Go Forward in So Great a Cause?*, BYU Women's Conference 2000

9 C.S. Lewis, Mere Christianity, page 176

10 C.S. Lewis, A Grief Observed, p21-22

11 Viktor E. Frankl, Man's Search for Meaning (New York: Washington Square Press, 1984), 87.

12 Vickey Pahnke, SheLovesGod.com Interview, September 2000

13 Marvin J. Ashton, "The Tongue Can Be a Sharp Sword," *Ensign*, May 1992

14 Vickey Pahnke, SheLovesGod.com Interview, September 2000

15 Ibid.

16 Ibid.

17 Ibid.

18 Ibid.

19 C.S. Lewis as quoted by Brent L. Top, *God's Megaphone to a Deaf World*, C.S. Lewis: The Man and His Message, p. 137-139)

20 Robert D. Hales, "The Covenant of Baptism: To Be in the Kingdom and of the Kingdom," *Ensign*, November 2000.

21 George Q. Cannon, Gospel Truth, Vol. 1, p.2

22 Virginia U. Jensen, *I Can Do All Things Through Christ*, The Best of Women's Conference, Bookcraft 2000, p. 234.

23 Sheri L. Dew, *As Women of God, Shall We Not Go Forward in So Great a Cause?*, BYU Women's Conference 2000

24 Sheri L. Dew, *Famous Last Words*, BYU Women's Conference 1999

25 Gordon B. Hinckley, Standing for Something, Times Books, 2000, p. 37

26 Jana Stanfield, *"That's the Way I Feel About You,"* *Brave Faith* 1999 Jana StanTunes Music, www.janastanfield.com.

27 Jenette Rotatori-Zubero, *So Who's Taking Care of You*, SheLovesGod.com Virtual Women's Conference, October 2000, www.LocateACoach.com.

28 Neal A. Maxwell, "Content with the Things Allotted unto Us," *Ensign,,* May 2000, 74

29 Sheri L. Dew, *Famous Last Words*, 1999 BYU Women's Conference

30 Ezra Taft Benson, "Born of God", *Ensign*, July 1989.

31 Marvin J. Ashton, "The Tongue Can Be A Sharp Sword," *Ensign*, May 1992

32 Sheri L. Dew, "Stand Tall and Stand Together," *Ensign*, November 2000.

33 Sheri L. Dew, *"This is a Test. It is Only a Test,"* BYU Women's Conference 1998

34 Words by Ralph Rodgers, Jr. and Music by K. Newell Dayley, *I Feel My Savior's Love*, 1979.

35 Sheri L. Dew, *Famous Last Words*, BYU Women's Conference 1999.

Resources

Contact the Author

C.E.S. Business Consultants
Attn: Marnie Pehrson
514 Old Hickory Ln.
Ringgold GA 30736 USA
ORDERS: 800-524-2307
Phone: 706-866-2295
Email: webmaster@SheLovesGod.com
http://www.pwgroup.com
http://www.IdeaMarketers.com
http://www.SheLovesGod.com

Books

Standing for Something: 10 Neglected Virtues That Will Heal Our Hearts and Homes
By Gordon B. Hinckley
ISBN 0-8129-3317-6

Home Management 101: A Guide for Busy Parents
By Debbie Williams
ISBN 1-891400-21-5
Available at http://www.organizedtimes.com

Music

Jana Stanfield
"Heavy Mental" music – music that inspires and uplifts.
http://www.JanaStanfield.com

Denise Davis
Inspired Christian music such as *"Eternally Grateful"*
http://www.DeniseDavis.com

Web Sites

SheLovesGod.com – Get your daily FAITH-lift
Read and write inspiring stories, poetry and articles. Join in
our Christian women's discussion list, message board and
weekly study lessons.
http://www.SheLovesGod.com

SheLovesGod.com Annual Virtual Women's Conference
A week of online chats, group telephone conferences, online
courses and articles for women of all denominations. Held
the 3rd week of October each year.
http://www.SheLovesGod.com/conference/

SheLovesGod.com Weekly Bible Study
http://www.SheLovesGod.com/study.cfm

MainStreetMom.com
The magazine for modern mothers with traditional values.
http://www.MainstreetMom.com

OrganizedTimes.com
Resources that give you more time...less stress...better quality of family life! http://www.OrganizedTimes.com

ParentingToolbox.com
Expert parenting advice for single, blended, divorced, step,
adopt, foster, and grandparent families
http://www.parentingtoolbox.com

About the Author

Marnie L. Pehrson, her husband Greg, and their six children live in North Georgia near Chattanooga, Tennessee. Marnie started her own home-based business in 1990, which eventually evolved into writing and developing niche-based Internet communities that help talented people discover, define, & deliver their message to the online world. She is the author of *How to Run a Successful Computer Training Business* and *Keeping Your Sanity in a Home Business*.

In February of 2000, at the urging of two close friends, Marnie opened SheLovesGod.com to share her love for the Savior and help bring women closer to Him. The site is designed to enlighten and uplift Christian women through inspirational articles, books and stories, and to give them a forum for strengthening each other. The goal of Marnie's weekly study lessons is to build the faith and spirituality of Christian women -- helping them reach their potential as daughters of God and fulfill their divine destinies. The home base of Marnie's projects is www.pwgroup.com. She welcomes reader comments at webmaster@shelovesgod.com.